THE
WORST-CASE
SCENARIO

SURVIVAL HANDBOOK

Expert Advice for
Extreme Situations

By Joshua Piven and David Borgenicht

CHRONICLE BOOKS
SAN FRANCISCO

Library of Congress Cataloging-in-Publication Data
Names: Piven, Joshua, author. | Borgenicht, David, author.
Title: The worst-case scenario survival handbook : expert
advice for extreme situations / by Joshua Piven and David
Borgenicht.
Description: San Francisco : Chronicle Books, [2019]
Identifiers: LCCN 2018061096 | ISBN 9781452172187
(hardcover : alk. paper)
Subjects: LCSH: Survival—Handbooks, manuals, etc. |
Survival—Humor.
Classification: LCC GF86 .P58 2019 | DDC 613.6/9—dc23
LC record available at https://lccn.loc.gov/2018061096

Manufactured in China.

Designed by Liam Flanagan.
Cover design by Neil Egan.
Cover illustration by Aurora Parlagreco.
Illustrations by Brenda Brown.

10 9 8 7 6 5 4 3

Chronicle Books LLC
680 Second Street
San Francisco, CA 94107
www.chroniclebooks.com

CONTENTS

Chapter Two
TOOTH AND CLAW

Chapter Three
THE BEST DEFENSE

Chapter Four
LEAPS OF FAITH

Chapter Five
TECHNICAL TROUBLE

Chapter Six
CRITICAL CONDITIONS

Chapter Seven
ADVENTURE SURVIVAL

FOREWORD

THE RULES OF SURVIVAL

By "Mountain" Mel Deweese

I am a Survival Evasion Resistance Escape Instructor. I have developed, written, attended, and taught courses around the world to more than 100,000 students—civilians, naval aviators, and elite Navy SEAL teams. I have more than 30 years of survival training experience, from the Arctic Circle to the Canadian wilderness, from the jungles of the Philippines to the Australian desert. Let's just say that I've learned a few things about survival over the years.

Whatever the situation, whether you're out in the mountains, on board a plane, or driving cross-country, to "survive" means "to outlive, to remain alive or in existence; live on. To continue to exist or live after." After all, that's what it's really all about—about continuing to exist, no matter how dire the circumstances.

- **You have to be prepared—mentally, physically, and equipment-wise.**

  I would have to call my training in the Arctic Circle the ultimate survival adventure. It's an extremely harsh and unforgiving environment, and yet the Inuit people not only survive, they live here at the top of the world. Most of the items you need for Arctic survival must come with you when you go—the Arctic offers little for improvisation.

One morning, as we huddled inside our igloo drinking warm tea, I noticed that our senior Inuit guide drank several more cups of tea than the rest of us. "He must be thirsty," I thought. After our morning trek across the frozen landscape and arrival at camp, the senior instructor walked over to a small knoll. Our young Inuit guide interpreted his words: "This is where the fox will come to seek a high lookout point. This is a good place to set a trap." The older man then took out his steel trap, set it, laid out the chain, and to my surprise, urinated upon the end of the chain, which froze solidly to the ground! The younger instructor explained: "That's why he drank all that tea this morning—to anchor it!"

The lesson: resources and improvisation equal survival.

- **You must not ignore the importance of the mental aspects of survival–in particular, stay calm and do not panic.**

   Remember that willpower is the most crucial survival skill of all—don't catch that terrible disease of "Giveup-itis." Mental strength especially come into play when someone, inevitably, makes a mistake.

   One trip into the jungles of the Philippines, our old guide Gunny gathered various plants while we were trekking. Once at the camp, Gunny skillfully prepared bamboo to use for cooking tubes. To these he added leaves, snails (old men catch snails because they are slow, he said, young men catch fast shrimp), and a few slices of green mango. He also added a few things I could not discern. Topping this off with some taro leaves, he added water and placed the cooking tubes on the fire.

After our jungle feast, we settled in to sleep. During the night, I experienced pain, contraction, and itching in my throat. We were in pitch darkness, far from civilization, and my airways were progressively closing. The following morning, the condition worsened. The instructor was experiencing the same problem, and this helped determine the source of our distress: we had not boiled the taro leaves long enough. Recovering hours later, I mentally logged this lesson, learned the hard way: even the old man of the jungle can make mistakes.

We all make mistakes. Overcoming them is survival.

- **You must have a survival plan that considers the following essential elements: food, fire, water, and shelter (as well as signals and first aid).**

A tropical environment is one of the easiest to survive. It offers all of the needs for survival—food, fire, water, shelter, if you know where to look. On a military survival training course in another jungle we needed water badly, but could not head for the major streams, rivers, or bodies of water, as the "enemy" was tracking us, and watching those areas. Looking into the foliage, our guide Pepe pointed with his jungle bolo (a large knife) to a thick, grapelike vine, three to four inches in diameter. He cut the vine at the top, then sliced off a two to three foot section, motioned to me, and held it above my parched lips. Excellent! It produced almost a large glass of water. Then he cut into a rattan vine that provided nearly the same amount. That evening we tapped into the trunk of a *taboy* tree, placed bamboo tube reservoirs we had constructed beneath the tap, and left them overnight. Early the next morning, there were six to eight quarts of water in our reservoirs.

The next morning in the rain, Pepe stopped to cut a tall bundle of grass. He wrapped the grass around a smoothbarked tree to form a spigot. He then placed his bamboo drinking cup underneath to gather rainwater. That night, after we had reached the safe area, the jungle darkness fell and we sat in the flicker of the fire. Pepe smiled at me and said, "Once again we've evaded the enemy and learned to return."

That simple phrase became our motto—and in fact, it is the motto of every survival trainer, whether or not they know it. "Learn to return."

This guide might help you do just that.

PREFACE

We have some good news, and some bad news.

The bad news first: We are sorry to report that it's still a dangerous world out there.

Despite our best efforts; despite the dramatic leaps we have taken forward in technology, medicine, and global awareness; despite the millions of readers we have reached over the past two decades with our handbooks (several of whom have claimed that their lives have been saved by our popular and entertaining-yet-accurate advice), danger still lurks beneath the surface, around the corner, and behind the door.

And you just never know when things might take a turn for the worse. Or the worst.

But here is the good news: We are STILL here to help.

When that moment comes, we want you to know what to do. We want you to know what to do when the pilot passes out, the train derails, or you start to sink in the quicksand. We want you to know what to do when the alligator attacks, the bull charges, or the clown looks more dangerous than fun. We want you to know what to do when your cell phone catches fire, when the levee breaks, or when you are buried alive.

Because it's being prepared that will save your life and your limb(s). But take heart—being prepared doesn't mean that you have to remember word for word what we tell you to do. Thankfully, the first key to surviving any worst-case scenario is simply this:

Do Not Panic.

So it's our hope, when the time comes, that having read this latest handy volume, you will know somewhere in the back of your brain that you have the answer to the question, "what the HELL do I do now?"—and that simple knowledge will be enough to keep you calm and cool, and give you the composure you need to make your move.

For this all-new, completely revised and updated edition, we've consulted firsthand with dozens of experts from all walks of life, to make sure that the advice is fully current and up to date with the latest techniques, advice, and information that could save your life, limbs, and loved ones. And we will continue to update this information at our website, www.worstcasescenario.com, as well as provide the latest survival info to help you handle whatever the world might throw your way.

Because it's still a dangerous world out there—but as always, and ever, we are here to help.

The Authors,
Joshua Piven and David Borgenicht

CHAPTER ONE

Great Escapes and Entrances

HOW TO BREAK DOWN A DOOR

INTERIOR DOORS

- Give the door a well-placed kick or two to the lock area to break it down.

  Kicking is more effective than running at the door and slamming against it—your foot exerts more force than your shoulder, and you will be able to direct this force toward the area of the locking mechanism more specifically.

Newer Construction

In newer construction, "contractor-grade" hollow-core doors may be primarily corrugated cardboard covered in vinyl, with only thin strips of wood along the edges. (Tap on the door; if it sounds hollow, it's cheap.) For these doors, a swift kick in the middle of one of the door "panels" should easily make a hole, allowing you to reach through and open it from the inside.

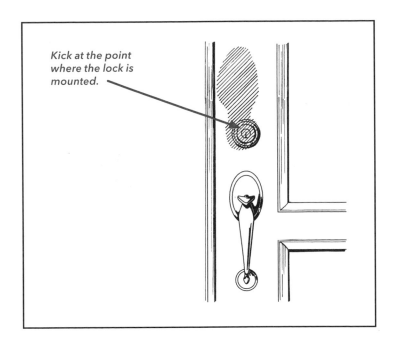

Kick at the point where the lock is mounted.

If You Have a Screwdriver

- **Probe the emergency access hole.**

  Look on the front of the doorknob for a small hole or keyhole. Most interior doors have what are called privacy sets. These locks are usually installed on bedrooms and bathrooms and can be locked from the inside when the door is shut, but have an emergency access hole in the center of the door handle that allows entry to the locking mechanism inside. Insert a thin screwdriver or probe into the handle and push the locking mechanism, or turn the mechanism to open the lock.

EXTERIOR DOORS

Breaking down an exterior door requires more force, as they are of sturdier construction and are designed with security in mind. You can generally expect to see two kinds of latches on outside doors: a knob lock for latching and light security, and a dead-bolt lock for added security. (On older homes they may be part of a single lockset called a thumb turn.) The knob lock keeps the door from swinging open, and will also keep the door handle from turning. The dead bolt set is used in conjunction with a knob lock and forces a steel bolt into the doorframe.

- **Give the door several well-placed kicks at the point where the lock is mounted.**

  An exterior door usually takes several tries to break down this way, so keep at it.

If You Have a Sturdy Piece of Steel

- **Remove the lock.**

  Wrench or pry the lock off the door by inserting the tool between the lock and the door and prying back and forth.

If You Have a Hammer and a Screwdriver or Awl

- **Remove the hinge pins.**

  Place the awl or screwdriver underneath the hinge, with the pointy end touching the end of the bolt or screw. Using the hammer, strike the other end of the awl or screwdriver until the hinge comes out. Remove the pins from the hinges and then force the door open from the hinge side. (The method works only on doors that open out.)

ASSESSING AMOUNT OF FORCE REQUIRED

Interior doors in general are of a lighter construction than exterior doors and usually are thinner—one and three-eighth inches thick to one and five-eighth inches thick—than exterior doors, which generally are one and three-quarter inches thick. Older homes will be more likely to have solid wood doors, while newer ones will have the cheaper, hollow-core models. Knowing what type of door you are dealing with will help you determine how to break it down. You can usually determine the construction and solidity of a door by tapping on it.

HOLLOW CORE This type is generally used only for interior doors, since it provides no insulation or security, and requires minimal force. These doors can often be opened with a screwdriver, or easily penetrated with a well-placed kick.

SOLID WOOD These are usually oak or some other hardwood, and require an average amount of force and a crowbar or other similar tool.

SOLID CORE These have a softwood inner frame with a laminate on each side and a chipped or shaved wood core, and require an average amount of force and a screwdriver.

METAL CLAD These are usually softwood with a thin metal covering, and require average or above average force and a crowbar.

HOLLOW METAL These doors are of a heavier gauge metal that usually has a reinforcing channel around the edges and the lock mounting area, and are sometimes filled with some type of insulating material. These require maximum force and a crowbar.

HOW TO LAND A PLANE

These instructions cover small passenger planes and jets (not commercial airliners).

1 If the plane has only one set of controls, push, pull, carry, or drag the pilot out of the pilot's seat.

2 Take your place at the controls.

3 Put on the radio headset.

Use the radio to call for help—there will be several control buttons on the yoke (the plane's steering wheel) or a CB-like microphone on the instrument panel. Depress the button to talk, release it to listen. Say "Mayday! Mayday! Mayday!" and give your situation, destination, and plane tail number, which should be printed on the top of the instrument panel. Say you have an emergency, there is no pilot, and you need to land as soon as possible.

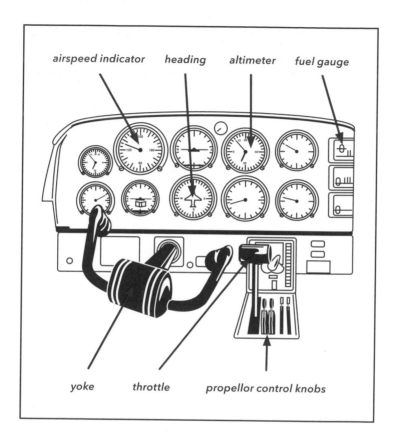

airspeed indicator   heading   altimeter   fuel gauge

yoke   throttle   propellor control knobs

4 **If you get no response, try again on the emergency channel—tune the radio to 121.50.**

All radios are different, but tuning is standard. The person on the other end should be able to talk you through the proper landing procedures. Follow their instructions carefully. If you cannot reach someone to talk you through the landing process, you will have to do it alone.

5 **Get your bearings and identify the instruments.**

Look around you. Is the plane level? Unless you have just taken off or are about to land, it should be flying relatively straight. If the autopilot is on, leave it on. If it is off, look for a blue button known as level-off. This newer technology automatically engages the autopilot and places the plane into a straight and level attitude.

YOKE This is the steering wheel and should be in front of you. It turns the plane and controls its pitch. Pull back on the column to bring the nose up, push forward to point it down. Turn left to turn the plane left, turn right to turn it right. The yoke is very sensitive—move it only an inch or two in either direction to turn the plane in flight. While cruising, the nose of the plane should be about three inches below the horizon for a person of average height. Measure using your fingers if necessary: the horizon should be about four to five finger widths above the cowling (hood) or glare-shield (dashboard) of the plane.

ALTIMETER This indicates the plane's altitude. It sits in the middle of the instrument panel and has three hands. The hand with the triangle at the tip indicates tens of thousands of feet, the widest hand indicates thousands of feet, and the long skinny hand indicates hundreds of feet.

HEADING This indicates direction of travel and will have a small image of a plane outlined in the center. The nose will point in the direction the plane is headed.

AIRSPEED This dial is on the top of the instrument panel, has colors, and will be on the left. It is usually calibrated in knots, though it may also have miles per hour. A small plane travels at about 120 knots while cruising. Anything under 50 knots in the air is dangerously close to stall speed. (A knot is one and a quarter miles per hour.)

THROTTLE This controls airspeed (power) and also the nose attitude, or its relation to the horizon. It is a lever between the seats and is always black. Pull it toward you to slow the plane and cause it to descend, push it away to speed up the plane and cause it to ascend. The engine will get more or less quiet depending on the direction the throttle is moved, just like a car.

FUEL The fuel gauges will be on the lower portion of the instrument panel. If the pilot has followed FAA regulations, the plane should have enough fuel for the amount of flying time to your intended destination, plus at least an additional half hour in reserve. Some planes have a reserve fuel tank in addition to the primary one, but do not worry about changing tanks.

FLAPS Due to their complexity, wing flaps can make the plane harder to control. Use the throttle, not the flaps, to control airspeed.

6 **Begin the descent.**

Pull back on the throttle to slow down. Reduce power by about one-quarter of cruising speed. As the plane slows, the nose will drop. For descent, the nose should be about four inches below the horizon, or five to six finger widths.

7 **Extend the landing gear.**

Determine if the plane has fixed or retractable landing gear. Fixed landing gear is always down so you don't need to do anything. If it is retractable, there will be another lever between the seats near the throttle, with a handle that is shaped like a tire. For a water landing, leave the landing gear up (retracted).

8 **Look for a suitable landing site.**

If you cannot find an airport, find a flat field on which to land. A mile-long field is ideal, but the plane can land on a much shorter strip of earth, so do not bother to look for the "perfect" landing site—there is no such thing. Bumpy terrain will also do if your options are limited. If there is an unoccupied beach, land close to the water's edge where the sand is firmer. If landing in water, land close to a boat or near shore, and keep the landing gear retracted. Never attempt to land a plane with fixed landing gear in water.

9 Line up the landing strip so that when the altimeter reads 1,000 feet, the field is off the right-wing tip.

In an ideal situation, you should take a single pass over the field to look for obstructions; with plenty of fuel, you may want to do so. Fly over the field, make a big rectangle, and approach a second time.

10 When approaching the landing strip, reduce power by pulling back on the throttle.

Do not let the nose drop more than six inches below the horizon.

11 The plane should be 100 feet off the ground when you are just above the landing strip, and the rear wheels should touch first.

The plane will aerodynamically stall—also called an airfoil or wing stall, distinct from the engine stalling—at 55–65 miles per hour/knots. You want the plane to be at just about stall speed when the wheels touch the ground.

12 Pull all the way back on the throttle, and make sure the nose of the plane does not dip too steeply.

Bring the nose up to meet the horizon. Gently pull back on the yoke as the plane slowly touches the ground.

13 **Using the pedals on the floor, steer and brake the plane as needed.**

The yoke has very little effect on the ground. The upper pedals are the brakes, and the lower pedals control the direction of the nose wheel. Concentrate first on the lower pedals. Press the right pedal to move the plane right, press the left pedal to move it left. Upon landing, be aware of your speed. A modest reduction in speed will increase your chances of survival exponentially. By reducing your groundspeed from 120 to 50–60 miles per hour/knots, you increase your chance of survival threefold.

PRO TIPS

▶   A well-executed emergency landing in bad terrain can be less hazardous than an uncontrolled landing on an established field.

▶   If the plane is headed toward trees, steer it between them so the wings absorb the impact if you hit.

▶   When the plane comes to a stop, get out as soon as possible and get away—and take the pilot with you.

▶   Move away from the plane toward the direction of the tail, and at least 15 feet beyond it.

▶   Most "six-pack" flight instrument layouts are as follows, from left to right. Top row: Airspeed, Attitude, Altimeter. Second row: Turn Coordinator, Heading, Vertical Speed.

HOW TO SURVIVE IN-FLIGHT EMERGENCIES

EXTREME TURBULENCE

1 **Secure all loose items.**

Turbulence may occur with little or no warning, causing anything not stowed to fly around the cabin. Keep any in-flight items you are not using—and particularly heavy items like books and electronics—in a closed bag, and place the bag under the seat in front of you or in the overhead bin. Put smaller items in the seat pocket. Do not leave potentially dangerous items (unopened cans of soda, for example) on your tray table.

2 **Fasten your seat belt.**

It should be as snug as possible without being uncomfortable. Extreme turbulence may cause sudden drops in the aircraft, resulting in unbelted passengers hitting the bottom of the overhead bins or the cabin ceiling, and causing severe injury.

3   **Raise the tray table.**

Make sure it is locked in place.

4   **Protect your head.**

Once you are safely belted into your seat, protect your head from projectiles. Hold a pillow, thick jacket, or folded blanket tightly over your head and face. If available, use an inflatable neck pillow to protect your neck. Do not use anything hard or heavy: if you lose your grip, it may become a projectile.

5   **Assume crash position.**

Lean over and put your head as close to your lap as possible while holding protective gear in place.

6   **Be alert for oxygen mask deployment.**

Oxygen masks are designed to drop upon changes in cabin pressure, but may deploy during turbulence. Do not panic if you see them released. Do not use one unless directed by the flight crew.

7   **Prepare for drops.**

Light to moderate turbulence can cause the aircraft to drop tens of feet, while more severe turbulence may result in hundred-foot drops, or potentially more. The pilot will typically try to avoid turbulent air by getting reports from preceding aircraft and changing altitude.

8   **Breathe through a bag.**

If you begin to hyperventilate, grab the air sickness bag, gather it at the top, bring it to your mouth, and inhale and exhale slowly through your mouth and into the bag. This procedure increases carbon dioxide levels in the blood, which may be depleted during hyperventilation. Note, however, that this solution may be dangerous if the hyperventilation is caused by a medical condition such as heart attack or asthma, not anxiety.

9   **Chat.**

In most cases, talking to a fellow passenger will promote more controlled breathing.

PRO TIPS

There are four classifications for turbulence.

- ▸ Light turbulence momentarily causes slight changes in altitude and/or attitude (roll, pitch, or yaw). You may feel slight strain against your seat belt, and objects might be slightly displaced.

- ▸ Moderate turbulence causes changes in altitude and attitude, but the pilot still maintains positive control of the aircraft. You will feel strain against the seat belt.

- ▸ Severe turbulence causes large, abrupt changes in altitude and/or attitude, and you will feel violent forces against the seat belt.

- ▸ Extreme turbulence causes the aircraft to be tossed about, making it impossible to control, and can result in structural damage.

Both severe and extreme turbulence may cause significant damage to the aircraft: if the sudden drops increase the load factor on the wings to a degree that exceeds the limits of the plane, the wings and other surfaces can be shorn off the fuselage.

TANTRUM CHILD

1 Move.

The more distance between you and the tantrum, the better. If the tantrum is already in progress during boarding, quickly scan the plane for potentially empty seats. When you spot one, immediately inform the flight attendant that you would like it. The instant you hear the aircraft door close, move. This strategy has its own risks: you may be crammed into a middle seat; behind an extreme seat recliner; closer to the lavatory and its constant foot traffic; or next to the passenger eating the sub with onions.

2 Use headphones.

Noise-canceling or other headphones may help to block out a screamer a few rows away, but are unlikely to work if the child is within a few seats. (The flight attendants may offer cheap headphones for a nominal fee if you don't have yours.) Over-ear headphones are more effective than ear buds.

Do not offer parenting advice. It is rarely appreciated.

3   **Make ear plugs.**

Chew two to four pieces of gum. When completely soft, form gum into two round balls, each approximately the size of a gumball. Rewrap the gum in foil wrappers and place one makeshift earplug over the opening of each ear, but not down the ear canal. Keep hair away from gum-plug.

4   **Use an inflatable neck pillow.**

Place a T-shirt on top of your head so each side hangs down over one ear. Take a neck pillow and place it on your head vertically: the bottom of the "u" should be against the crown of your head, with the sides against your ears, holding the T-shirt in place. Close your eyes and imagine your happy place.

5 **Consider alcohol.**

A few stiff cocktails may help you pass out.

PRO TIP

Do not offer parenting advice. It is rarely appreciated.

EXTREME SEAT RECLINER

Take the following steps, in order, to deal with a passenger in front of you who fully reclines their seat.

1 **Try kindness.**

Tap the extreme recliner on the shoulder and politely ask if they would mind moving the seat-back forward. While doing so, shift your body so your knees are pressed against the seat-back (if they aren't already) to demonstrate your severe discomfort.

2 **Try kindness combined with lying.**

During your ask, note that you're recovering from knee surgery and the seat-back pressing against your kneecap has you ready to pass out from the pain. Offer to show the extreme recliner your (fake) scar.

3 **Borrow a lap child.**

Place someone else's infant on your lap, then make your ask. Return the infant when the seat-back has been moved up.

4   **Surreptitiously move the seat-back up.**

When the extreme recliner gets up to use the lavatory, reach into their row, depress the button, and move the seat-back forward slightly. (Do not attempt to move it to its full upright position or the recliner will notice and move it right back). If the extreme recliner is not in the aisle seat, or has traveling companions, you may need to create a diversion first. Try dropping a cup of water in the aisle next to their row, then make your move when passengers turn to see what happened.

5   **Use the knee maneuver, but only as a last resort.**

Purposely ramming your knees into the seat back to make your discomfort clear to the extreme recliner may result in an argument or, if alcohol is involved, a fist fight. Regular extreme recliners are well versed in this strategy, and are willing to put up with the occasional knee-in-the-back for the added comfort of a full recline.

6   **Do not fully recline your own seat.**

You will only be adding to the problem, and this solution does nothing to protect your knees from the full recline in front of you.

PRO TIP

Purpose-built devices to prevent aircraft seat recline may be available, but may be prohibited by some airlines.

SNAKES ON THE PLANE

1 **Do not scream.**

While a snake cannot "hear" in the traditional sense, snakes are highly attuned to their environment: the inner ear is very sensitive and transmits vibrations to the brain, and may also convert sound waves to vibrations. Screaming may disturb the snakes and make them more aggressive.

2 **Lift your feet up.**

Snakes require warm objects to help regulate body temperature. They will naturally move away from cooler areas of the plane—including the floor and any metal objects in contact with it—and toward warmer places, such as passengers or the galley ovens (on international flights that include meals).

3 **Turn the reading light on.**

Many harmless, nonvenomous snakes see very well in daylight. However, venomous pit vipers (rattlesnakes, bushmasters) have infrared sensors that detect body heat, allowing them to navigate and attack in complete darkness. Dimming reading and cabin lights will make navigating the plane more difficult for you, but not for these snakes.

4 **Lower the tray table.**

The tray table will give snakes a sturdy surface on which to climb.

5 **Limit your movement.**

If you must leave (or return to) your seat, move very slowly. A snake will react in milliseconds if it senses any action that it may perceive as a threat, which includes fast, jerky motions or movements.

6 **Do not grab the tail.**

A snake will immediately turn and bite the hand that grabs at its tail; you will not be able to grasp the tail and toss the snake into another row before it bites you.

7 **Allow the snakes to crawl over or climb up you.**

If you cannot get away from the snakes, your best option is to remain still as the snake or snakes move over/across you and into another row.

8 **Support the snake.**

A snake that feels comfortable and secure is less likely to attack. Once the snake has climbed on you, carefully support its weight so it does not fall. Even if it appears the snake is dropping to the floor, do not pull on it: support the part of its body that is still on yours and let it navigate on its own. Slowly place your arm on the tray table to allow the snake to move onto it.

How to Capture Snakes

It may be possible to trap snakes in either the lavatory or in overhead bins. Note, however, that the snakes will need to move to these areas naturally, on their own. If it is safe to do so, open overhead bins and the doors to the lavatories and, once snakes enter, close the doors.

PRO TIP

The first-class lavatory is for first-class passengers only.

HOW TO BREAK INTO A CAR

Depending on make, many cars built in the last 20 years use key fobs and encrypted electronic communication protocols to unlock the doors. However, even these cars typically have a manual, mechanical override in the event there is an electronics failure. Cars with vertical, push-button locks are the easiest to open. These are locks that come straight out of the top of the car door and have rods that are set vertically inside the door. These locks can be easily opened with a wire hanger or a lockout tool, or picked. Horizontal locks that emerge from the side of the car door and are attached to horizontal lock rods are difficult to see from outside the door and more difficult to manipulate without a special tool, but they can also be picked. (We of course assume you are seeking to enter your own car.)

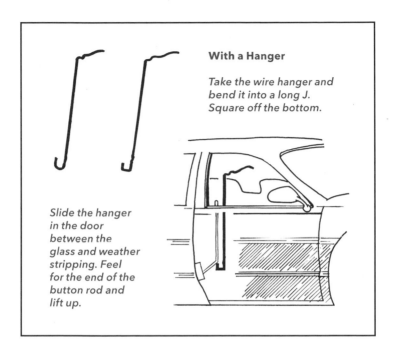

With a Hanger

Take the wire hanger and bend it into a long J. Square off the bottom.

Slide the hanger in the door between the glass and weather stripping. Feel for the end of the button rod and lift up.

WITH A HANGER

1 Take a wire hanger and bend it into a long J.

2 Square off the bottom of the J so the square is one and one-half inch to two inches wide.

3 Slide the hanger into the door, between the window and the weather stripping.

Open the door by feel and by trial and error. Feel for the end of the button rod and, when you have it, pull it up to open the lock.

WITH A LOCKOUT TOOL

A lockout tool is a thin piece of spring steel with a notch in one side, which makes it easy to pull the lock rod up, or move it sideways. They come in various lengths and thicknesses for different makes of car, and can be purchased online or at most automotive supply stores.

1 **Slide the tool gently between the window and the weather stripping.**

Some cars will give you only a quarter of an inch of access to the lock linkage, so go slowly and be patient.

With a Lockout Tool

Slide the device between the glass and the weather stripping. Feel for the lock rod. Move the tool back and forth gently until the lock flips over.

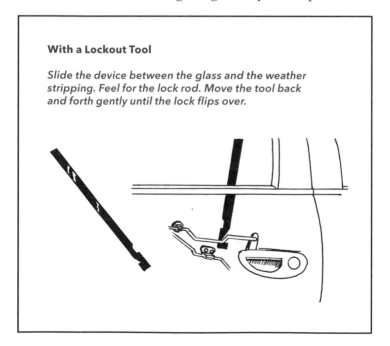

2 **Do not jerk the tool trying to find the lock rod.**
This can break the lock linkage, and on electronic locks it can easily rip the wires in the door.

3 **Move the tool back and forth until it grabs the lock rod, and then gently move it back and forth until the lock flips over.**

PRO TIP

Newer cars may contain thin steel plates in the doors to prevent the use of a lockout tool. And virtually all car doors are now filled with wiring and airbags. Use caution when attempting to unlock the door with a lockout tool, as costly damage may result.

HOW TO PICK A DOOR LOCK

Modern car locks no longer use pins: most use wafers, which are similar to pins, or sliders. Wafer locks can be identified by the notching or "biting" on the blade of the key, while slider locks have a snake-like cutout on each side, running down the middle of the blade. Both types can be opened using a pick and tension wrench. Wafer locks can also be picked using a "jiggler," which resembles a key but is wavy and snake-like and the same length as the original, or by a specialized metal tool (a rake or scrubber) in place of a traditional pick.

If you don't have a jiggler or rake/scrubber, you will need two tools—the pick to manipulate the wafers or sliders inside the lock core, and a tension tool to turn the cylinder once they are aligned. In a pinch, you can use a small Allen wrench to turn the lock and a long bobby pin to move the wafers. Specialized lock pick sets for autos are also available online and will make things easier. Keep in mind that many car locks are harder to pick than door locks. They often have a small shutter that covers and protects the lock, and this can make the process more difficult.

1   **While the bobby pin or pick is in the lock, exert constant and light turning pressure with the wrench.**
This is the only way to discern if the wafers or sliders—which line up with the notches and grooves in a key—are lined up correctly. Most locks have five wafers/sliders.

2   **Move the bobby pin to manipulate the wafers/sliders as you exert turning pressure with the tension wrench until you feel the lock turn smoothly.**

PRO TIP

Use a key from a different car from the same manufacturer. The alien key just may work. This trick is mostly applicable to older cars, and you may need to use a rubber mallet to force the key into the lock cylinder to align the wafers.

HOW TO PERFORM A FAST 180-DEGREE TURN WITH YOUR CAR

FROM REVERSE

1   Put the car in reverse and put your left hand at the six o'clock position on the wheel.

2   Select a spot straight ahead.

Keep your eyes on it, and begin backing up.

3   Jam on the gas.

Hold it for a count of three.

4   Drop the transmission into neutral and whip the wheel quickly around to the nine o'clock position (three-quarters of a turn).

Make sure you have enough speed to use the momentum of the car to swing it around, but stay below 45 miles per hour, or you may flip the car (and strip your gears). Turning the wheel left will swing the rear of the car left; turning it right will swing the car right.

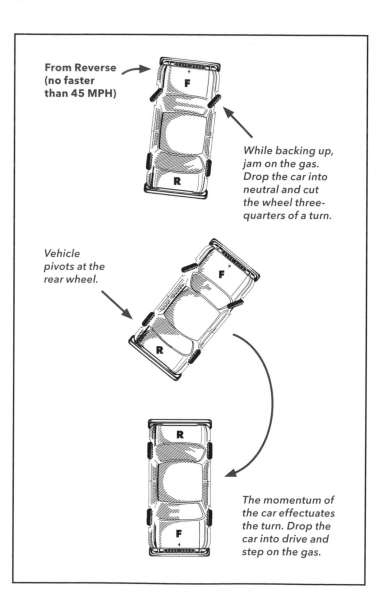

From Reverse (no faster than 45 MPH)

While backing up, jam on the gas. Drop the car into neutral and cut the wheel three-quarters of a turn.

Vehicle pivots at the rear wheel.

The momentum of the car effectuates the turn. Drop the car into drive and step on the gas.

5 When the car has completed the turn, drop the car into drive, step on the gas, and drive off.

FROM DRIVE

1 Accelerate to a moderate rate of speed.

While in drive or another forward gear, accelerate to a moderate rate of speed (anything faster than 45 miles per hour risks flipping the car).

2 Slip the car into neutral.

This should prevent the front wheels from spinning.

3 Take your foot off the gas and turn the wheel slightly in the opposite direction you want to turn.

4 Then quickly turn the wheel one-half turn in the direction you want to go while pulling hard on the emergency brake.

5 As the rear swings around, return the wheel to its original position.

6 Release the emergency brake and put the car back into drive.

7 Step on the gas to start moving in the direction from which you came.

PRO TIPS

▸ The 180-degree turn while moving forward is more difficult; it is easier to swing the heavier front of the car around, and it is harder to maintain control of the lighter rear of the car.

▸ Road conditions can play a significant role in the success—and safety—of this maneuver. Any surface without sufficient traction (dirt, mud, ice, gravel) will make quick turns harder and collisions more likely.

▸ A wet road makes these maneuvers much easier, but makes controlling the car more difficult.

HOW TO
RAM A CAR

Ramming a car to move it out of your way is not easy or safe, but if it is necessary, some methods are better than others. It's best to clip the very rear of the obstacle car, about one foot from the rear bumper—the rear of the car is lighter and easier to move.

1 **Disable your airbag, if you can.**

It will deploy on impact and will temporarily obstruct your view after it deploys, but it will deflate quickly.

2 **Fasten your seat belt.**

3 **Accelerate to at least 25 miles per hour.**

Do not go too fast—a slow speed on approach will allow you to maintain control without slowing down.

4 **Increase speed just before impact.**

Increase your speed to greater than 30 miles per hour.

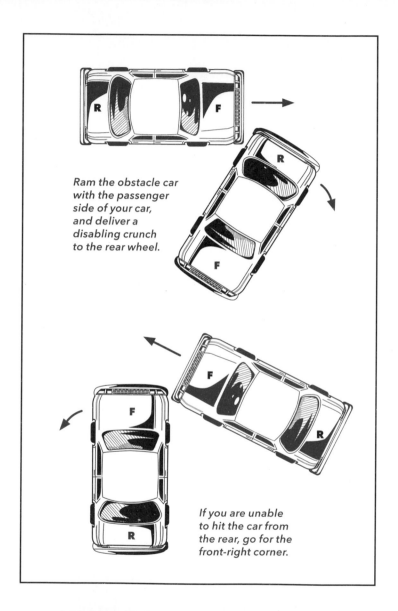

Ram the obstacle car with the passenger side of your car, and deliver a disabling crunch to the rear wheel.

If you are unable to hit the car from the rear, go for the front-right corner.

5   Ram the front passenger side of your car into the obstacle car at its rear wheel, at a 90-degree angle.

The cars should be perpendicular or as close as possible when you hit.

6   If unable to hit the rear, go for the front corner.

Avoid hitting the car squarely in the side; this will not move it out of your way.

7   Hit the gas and keep moving.

The car should spin out of your way.

PRO TIPS

▶   Newer cars may have safety features that turn the engine off when the car's computer sees that an airbag has deployed. In most cases, turning the ignition off and then back on will allow you to get underway.

▶   Hitting it in the rear can also disable the car—with the rear wheel crushed, you have time to get away without being pursued.

HOW TO SURVIVE A CAR CRASH

1   **Brake early and keep braking.**

The impact of sudden deceleration causes most car injuries and fatalities. The more you can reduce your speed before impact, the better your chances of survival.

2   **Sit back in the seat.**

The farther you are from an inflating airbag, the greater its effectiveness in slowing you down in a collision. The force of airbags is greatest in the instant they inflate.

3   **Keep your seat belt fastened.**

Seat belt webbing stretches while holding you in the seat, preventing sudden deceleration and keeping you from becoming a projectile.

4   **Keep legs and hands away from airbags.**

For drivers, keep thumbs and forearms away from the steering wheel airbag. For passengers, keep arms and, especially, legs off the dash. Airbags may cause serious injury to extremities as they inflate.

5 **Avoid broadside collisions.**

There is less protection of the passenger compartment on the sides of the car frame than in the front or rear (the "crumple zones"), and often fewer airbags. If you cannot avoid a crash, the front of the car provides more distance between you and the other vehicle or object.

6 **Swerve, but only at low speeds.**

Sudden inputs to the steering wheel at high speeds will cause the car to veer sharply, and overcorrection after veering may cause a rollover. Do not swerve until the car is moving below about 40 miles per hour.

7 **Steer right.**

If a head-on collision is imminent, brake and steer to the right. Steering to the left may help you avoid an initial collision, but you risk being hit by a second car moving in the same direction as the first.

8 **Aim for grass.**

Move the car off the road and onto a forgiving surface as you slow down. Avoid immobile objects, such as trees.

PRO TIPS

▶ Avoid driving between midnight and 2 a.m. on Friday and Saturday nights, when other drivers may be impaired.

▶ Avoid driving in the left lane on the interstate, especially at night. Drivers traveling in the wrong direction will usually be in this lane.

HOW TO ESCAPE FROM A SINKING CAR

1   Open your window as soon as you hit the water.

This is your best chance of escape, because opening the door will be very difficult given the outside water pressure. (To be safe, you should drive with the windows open whenever you are near water; when driving on ice, keep doors slightly open as well.) Opening the windows allows water to come in and equalize the pressure. Once the water pressure inside and outside the car is equal, you'll be able to open the door.

2   Break the glass.

Power windows may work at first, until the car's electronics get wet. If you cannot open them, break the glass with your foot or a sharp object, focusing on the edge of the glass, not the center. Tempered glass is easiest to break via a small point of contact, such as the metal edge of the seat belt buckle.

3   Get out.

Get out as soon as possible, while the car is still afloat. Depending on the vehicle, floating time will range from

As soon as you hit the water, open the windows. Otherwise, the pressure of the water will make it very difficult to escape. If you were unable to open a window before hitting the water, attempt to break one with your foot or a sharp object.

a few seconds to a few minutes. The more airtight the car, the longer it floats. Air in the car will quickly be forced out through the trunk and cab, and an air bubble is unlikely to remain once the car hits bottom. Vehicles with engines in front will sink at a steep angle. If the water is 15 feet or deeper, the vehicle may end up on its roof, upside down.

4 **If trapped inside, wait until the car fills with water.**

Remain calm and do not panic. Wait until the car begins filling with water. When the water reaches your head, take a deep breath and hold it. Now the pressure should be equalized inside and outside, and you should be able to open the door and swim to the surface.

HOW TO AVOID BREAKING THROUGH THE ICE

- ▸ Cars and light trucks need at least eight inches of clear, solid ice on which to drive safely.

- ▸ Avoid driving on ice early or late in the season.

- ▸ Leaving your car in one place for a long period of time can weaken the ice beneath it.

- ▸ Cars should not be parked—or driven—close together.

- ▸ Cross any cracks at right angles, and drive slowly.

- ▸ New ice is generally thicker than old ice.

- ▸ Direct freezing of lake or stream water is stronger than refreezing, freezing of melting snow, or freezing of water bubbling up through cracks.

- ▸ A layer of snow on the ice can insulate it, slowing the freezing process. The snow's weight can also decrease the bearing capacity of the ice.

- ▸ Ice near the shore is weaker.

- ▸ River ice is generally weaker than lake ice.

- ▸ River mouths are dangerous, because the ice near them is weaker.

HOW TO
SURVIVE A TRAIN
DERAILMENT

1 **Listen for the train horn.**

If a forward collision is imminent, you may hear a repeated series of short whistles as the operator warns of the train's approach. You will have just seconds to act.

2 **Don't jump.**

You're more likely to be injured by an obstacle near the track bed than by the collision.

3 **Move to a seat in a passenger car.**

Quickly get out of the café car, the bathroom, or the space between cars; these areas present greater danger of injury during a collision. If you are lying down in a roomette, stay there. If time permits, move as far back in the car (or on the train) as possible. If the train is a push-pull (locomotives front and rear), the rear locomotive will have more robust brakes than passenger cars and may act as an "anchor" to help slow the train.

4 **Locate a "zip strip" window.**

Train car windows are extremely durable and shatterproof, and may provide the only means for rescuers to reach you. Choose a seat with a window containing a "zip strip," the rubber grommet with an emergency release handle used to open the window.

5 **Brace for impact.**

Keep your body below the level of the headrest. Use clothing or blankets to protect your head and prepare for impact. Hold tightly to the seat arms. Passenger railcars do not have seat belts.

6 **Prepare for the accordion effect.**

The tracks and track bed will absorb much of the impact, and the tightlock couplers will minimize lateral forces and keep cars upright in most cases. Moving trains don't stop immediately, however, and passenger cars may end up in a zigzag orientation, called the accordion effect. You may feel the car moving or sliding sideways.

7 **Wait until the train stops moving.**

Check yourself and other passengers for injury.

8 **Check for smoke.**

Diesel-electric locomotives run on diesel fuel, and there is risk of fire in a collision. Some cars may have a fire extinguisher near either end. Use it if needed.

9 **Listen for instructions.**

If present, a conductor or other railroad employee will advise you on evacuation procedures.

10 **Evacuate if necessary.**

If flames are present or the train is taking on water, exit the car by crawling through a window. There may be significant risk of electrocution from the catenary system, which powers electric locomotives and is as dangerous as high-tension wires. Do not assume that power has been cut off.

PRO TIP

Keep clear of parallel tracks: trains may be approaching the crash site and unable to slow or stop.

HOW TO SURVIVE BEING BURIED ALIVE

1   **Conserve your air supply.**

If you are buried in a typical coffin, you will have enough air to survive for an hour or two at most. Take deep breaths, and then hold for as long as possible before exhaling. Do not breathe and then swallow, which will lead to hyperventilation. Do not light a match or lighter. Combustion will quickly use your available oxygen. It is safe to use a flashlight if you have one. Do not yell. Yelling will lead to panic, which will increase your heart rate and lead to fast breathing that will rapidly consume your air supply.

2   **Press up on the coffin lid with your hands.**

An inexpensive "pine box" (chipboard coffin) or a recycled paperboard coffin will have some give to it, so it will be relatively easy to break through. If you feel flex in the coffin lid, continue to step 3. A metal-clad or hardwood coffin will be impossible to pierce. In this case, your only hope is to signal for rescue. Use a metal object (ring, belt buckle, coin, flask, pen) to signal that you are alive. Tap SOS, the international distress signal, on the coffin lid: three quick taps, followed by three slower taps, followed by three quick taps. Continue to repeat the distress call until someone hears you.

3   **Remove your shirt.**

Cross your arms over your chest, and then uncross your arms so that your elbows are bent and your hands are at your shoulders. Pull your shirt up and off your head from the shoulders, do a partial sit-up (as much as you can in the space available), and then pull your shirt over your head and off.

4   **Tie the bottom of the shirt in a knot.**

The shirt should have only one large opening, at the neck, as does a bag.

5   **Place your head through the neck hole.**

The knot should be on the top of your head. The shirt will prevent you from suffocating on loose earth.

6   **Break through the coffin.**

Using your feet, begin kicking the coffin lid. A cheap coffin may have already split from the weight of the earth above, making your job easier. Break apart the lid with your hands and feet, and let the loose dirt rush in.

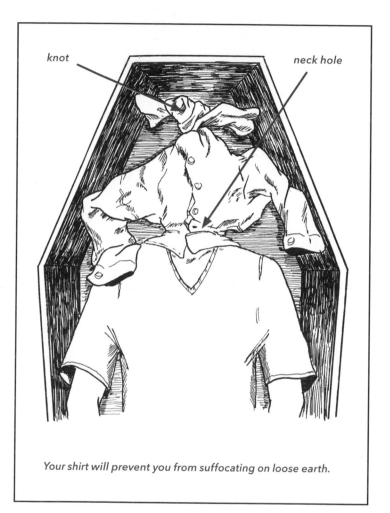

knot

neck hole

Your shirt will prevent you from suffocating on loose earth.

7 **Use your hands to push the dirt toward your feet.**

There should be some space at the bottom end of the coffin, below your feet. As the dirt rushes in, work quickly but calmly to fill the space at your feet. When this space fills up, push dirt to your sides. Breathe slowly and regularly.

8 **Sit up.**

As you move to a seated position, the loose earth above will move to fill the space you just occupied. As the dirt falls, continue to push it into the coffin until you can stand up.

9 **Stand.**

Once you are standing, you should be able to push the dirt above you up and out of the grave. When you have cleared all the dirt above you, climb out.

PRO TIPS

▸ A recently interred coffin will be covered with loose earth that is relatively easy to dig through.

▸ Escaping from a coffin interred during a rainstorm will be difficult. The compacted weight of the wet earth will make digging almost impossible.

▸ The higher the clay content of the soil, the more difficult your escape will be.

CHAPTER TWO

Tooth and Claw

HOW TO SURVIVE A SNAKE ATTACK

HOW TO TREAT A BITE

1 Wash the bite with soap and water.

2 Immobilize the bitten area and keep it lower than the heart.

This will slow the flow of the venom.

3 Get medical help as soon as possible.

A doctor should treat all snakebites unless you are willing to bet your life that the offending snake is nonvenomous. Of about 8,000 venomous bites a year in the United States, 9 to 15 victims are killed. A bite from any type of venomous snake should always be considered a medical emergency.

4 Wrap a bandage.

Immediately tightly wrap a bandage two to four inches above the bite to help slow the venom. The bandage should not cut off blood flow from a vein or artery. Make the bandage loose enough for a finger to slip underneath.

*Snakes coil
before they strike.*

*Snakes can strike at approximately
half their length; half their body
does not leave the ground.*

5 **Use a suction device on the venom.**

If you have a first aid kit equipped with a suction device, follow the instructions to place the rubber suction cup over the bite marks and draw venom out of the wound without making an incision. Do not attempt to suck out the venom—if it is in your mouth, it can enter your bloodstream.

WHAT NOT TO DO

- ▶ Do not place any ice or cooling element on the bite; this will make removing the venom with suction more difficult.

- ▶ Do not tie a bandage or a tourniquet too tightly. If used incorrectly, a tourniquet can cut blood flow completely and damage the limb.

- ▶ Do not make any incision on or around the wound in an attempt to remove the venom—it may become infected.

PRO TIPS

▶ Because venomous snakes can be difficult to identify—and because some nonvenomous snakes have markings very similar to venomous ones—the best way to avoid getting bitten is to leave all snakes alone. Assume that a snake is venomous unless you know for certain that it is not.

▶ Even bites from nonvenomous snakes should be treated professionally, as severe allergic reactions can occur. Some Mojave rattlesnakes carry a neurotoxic venom that can affect the brain or spinal cord, causing paralysis.

HOW TO ESCAPE FROM A PYTHON

Unlike venomous snakes, pythons and boas kill their prey not through the injection of venom but by constriction (hence they are known as constrictors). A constrictor coils its body around its prey, squeezing it until the pressure is great enough to kill.

1 **Move slowly.**

Moving energetically against the python will cause the snake to tighten its grip. But do not remain still and play dead, as a python usually continues constricting well after the prey is dead and not moving.

2 **Control the head.**

With one hand, grasp the python's head to immobilize it.

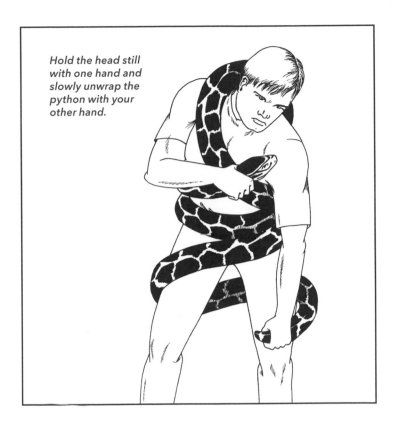

Hold the head still with one hand and slowly unwrap the python with your other hand.

3 **Unwrap the coils.**

With the other hand, hold the python's tail and bend away from you to unwrap the coils.

4 **Stun the snake.**

If the python continues to constrict and you cannot escape, strike it firmly on the center of its head to stun it temporarily and continue to uncoil.

PRO TIPS

- Pythons and boas can grow to be 20 feet long, and are capable of killing a grown person; small children are even more vulnerable.

- Most pythons will strike and then try to get away, rather than consume a full-grown human.

HOW TO AVOID AN ATTACK

- Do not approach, prod, try to move, or try to kill a snake.

- If you come across a snake, back away slowly and give it a wide berth: snakes can easily strike half their body length in an instant, and some species measure six feet or longer.

- When hiking in an area with venomous snakes, always wear thick leather boots and long pants.

- Keep to marked trails.

- Be aware that snakes are cold-blooded and need the sun to help regulate their body temperature. They are often found lying on warm rocks or in other sunny places.

HOW TO FEND OFF A SHARK

1 **Stay Calm**

If a shark approaches you, it is probably simply curious: large sharks are primarily stealth predators and will typically not show themselves prior to an attack.

2 **Hit the eyes or gills.**

If the shark attacks you, use anything you have—a camera, a probe, a harpoon gun, your fist—to hit the shark's eyes or gills, the areas most sensitive to pain.

3 **Make quick, sharp, repeated jabs.**

As predators, sharks will usually follow through on an attack only if they have the advantage, so making the shark unsure of its advantage in any way possible will increase your chances of survival. Contrary to popular opinion, the shark's nose is not the area to attack, unless you cannot reach the eyes or gills. Hitting the shark simply tells it that you are not defenseless.

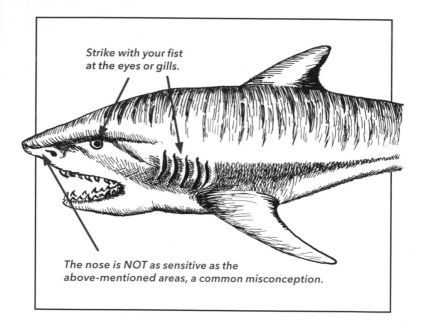

Strike with your fist at the eyes or gills.

The nose is NOT as sensitive as the above-mentioned areas, a common misconception.

HOW TO AVOID AN ATTACK

- **Always stay in groups.**

  Sharks are more likely to attack an individual.

- **Do not wander too far from shore.**

  This isolates you and creates the additional danger of being too far from assistance.

- **Avoid being in the water during darkness or twilight hours.**

  Sharks are most active and have a competitive sensory advantage in low light.

- **Do not enter the water if you are bleeding from an open wound or if you are menstruating.**
  Sharks are drawn to the smell of blood, and their olfactory ability is acute.

- **Do not wear shiny jewelry.**
  The reflected light resembles the sheen of fish scales.

- **Avoid waters with known effluence or sewage and those being used by sport or commercial fishermen, especially if there are signs of baitfish or feeding activity.**
  Diving seabirds are good indicators of such activity.

- **Use extra caution when waters are murky.**
  Avoid showing any uneven tan lines or wearing brightly colored clothing—sharks see contrast particularly well.

- **If a shark shows itself to you, it may be curious rather than predatory.**
  It will probably swim on and leave you alone. If you are under the surface and lucky enough to see an attacking shark, then you do have a good chance of defending yourself if the shark is not too large.

- **Scuba divers should avoid lying on the surface.**
  They may look like a piece of prey to a shark, and from there they cannot see a shark approaching.

- **A shark attack is a potential danger for anyone who frequents marine waters, but it should be kept in perspective.**

  Bees, wasps, and snakes are responsible for far more fatalities each year than sharks, and in the United States the annual risk of death from lightning is 30 times greater than from a shark attack.

THREE KINDS OF SHARK ATTACKS

"HIT AND RUN" ATTACKS These are the most common, and typically occur in the surf zone, where swimmers and surfers are the targets. The victim seldom sees the attacker, and the shark does not return after inflicting a single bite or slash wound.

"BUMP AND BITE" ATTACKS The shark initially circles and often bumps the victim prior to the actual attack. These types of attacks usually involve divers or swimmers in deeper waters, but also occur in nearshore shallows in some areas of the world.

"SNEAK" ATTACKS These can occur without warning. With both "bump and bite" and "sneak" attacks, repeat attacks are common, and multiple and sustained bites are the norm. Injuries incurred during this type of attack are usually quite severe, frequently resulting in death.

PRO TIPS

- Most shark attacks occur in nearshore waters, typically inshore of a sandbar or between sandbars, where sharks feed and can become trapped at low tide.

- Areas with steep drop-offs are also likely attack sites. Sharks congregate in these areas, because their natural prey congregates there.

- Most at risk are surfers and spear fishermen. Surfers venture beyond the backline of waves where the water is deep. Point breaks are often risky surfing areas, as the water rapidly becomes deep in these areas. Spear fishers venture out to hunt fish in the same areas where sharks are hunting.

- Almost any large shark, roughly six feet or longer in total length, is a potential threat to humans. But three species in particular have repeatedly attacked man: the white shark (*Carcharodon carcharias*), the tiger shark (*Galeocerdo cuvier*), and the bull shark (*Carcharhinus leucas*). All are cosmopolitan in distribution, reach large sizes, and consume large prey such as marine mammals, sea turtles, and fish as normal elements of their diets.

HOW TO ESCAPE FROM A BEAR

HOW TO PREVENT AN ATTACK

1   **Stand tall.**

Stand at full height in a neutral stance. Do not crouch or threaten. Keep your eyes on the bear.

2   **Demonstrate that you are not a threat.**

Speak softly using an appeasing tone. Bears may naturally assume a human will attack them, and are able to assess intent. It is critical to show the bear that you are not a threat.

IF THE BEAR CHARGES

A bear may "bluff" charge, running at you and then stopping and backing away. Bluff charging is common bear behavior, and its meaning and intent are contextual: the intensity of the charge may reflect how stressed the bear is.

If the bear charges, be ready to defend yourself, but do not assume the bear will attack until you have actually been taken off your feet.

1 **Strike back at the eyes or snout.**

Once you are under attack, strike back with anything you can. Go for the bear's eyes or its snout.

WHAT TO DO IF YOU SEE A BEAR

- ▶ Make your presence known by talking loudly, clapping, singing, or calling out. (Some hikers wear bells while in bear country.) Be heard, and avoid surprising a bear.

- ▶ Keep children close at hand and within sight.

- ▶ There is no guaranteed minimum safe distance from a bear: the farther, the better.

- ▶ If you are in a car, remain in your vehicle. Do not get out, even for a quick photo. Keep your windows up. Do not impede the bear from crossing the road.

HOW TO AVOID AN ATTACK

▶ Reduce or eliminate food odors from yourself, your camp, your clothes, and your vehicle.

▶ Do not sleep in the same clothes you cook in.

▶ Store food so that bears cannot smell or reach it.

▶ Do not keep food in your tent—not even a chocolate bar.

▶ Properly store and bring out all garbage.

▶ Handle and store pet food with as much care as your own.

▶ While all bears should be considered dangerous and avoided, three types should be regarded as more dangerous than the average bear:

- Females defending cubs

- Bears habituated to human food

- Bears defending a fresh kill

PRO TIPS

▶ Do not climb a tree to escape a bear. Bears can climb trees easily and will come after you, although black bears are better tree-climbers than grizzly bears.

▶ Bears can run as fast as horses, uphill or downhill.

▶ Bears have excellent senses of smell and hearing.

▶ Bears are extremely strong. They can tear cars apart looking for food.

*While all bears are dangerous,
these three situations are especially dangerous:*

*Bears habituated
to human food*

*Females
protecting cubs*

*Bears defending
a fresh kill*

- Every bear defends a "personal space." The extent of this space will vary with each bear and each situation; it may be as few as six feet or as large as a thousand feet. Intrusion into this space is considered a threat and may provoke an attack.

- Bears aggressively defend their food.

- All female bears defend their cubs. If a female with cubs is surprised at close range or is separated from her cubs, she may attack.

- An aggressive reaction to any danger to her cubs is the mother grizzly's natural defense.

- A female black bear's natural defense is to chase her cubs up a tree and defend them from the base.

- Stay away from dead animals. Bears may attack to defend such food.

- It is best not to hike with dogs in bear country, as dogs can antagonize bears and cause an attack. An unleashed dog may even bring a bear back to you.

HOW TO ESCAPE FROM A MOUNTAIN LION

1 **Stand still.**

If you spot the mountain lion from a distance, before it spots you, stay completely still. Running will simply cause it to pay more attention.

2 **Observe its behavior.**

Mountain lions are stealth, ambush hunters that attack prey from close range, typically from a distance of 15-30 feet. If the lion is ahead of you and has its attention focused elsewhere, do not do anything to attract it.

3 **Make yourself appear bigger.**

If the mountain lion has spotted you, try to make yourself appear bigger by opening your coat wide. The mountain lion is less likely to attack a larger animal.

4 **Do not crouch down.**

Hold your ground, wave your hands, and shout. Show it that you are not defenseless. Do all you can to appear larger. If you have a walking stick or other stout pole, hold it at the ready.

Upon sighting a mountain lion, do not run. Do not crouch down. Try to make yourself appear larger by opening your coat wide.

5 **If you have small children with you, pick them up.**
Children, who move quickly and have high-pitched voices, are at higher risk than adults.

6 **Back away slowly or wait until the animal moves away.**
Report any lion sightings to authorities as soon as possible.

7 **If the lion still behaves aggressively, throw stones.**
Convince the lion that you are not prey and that you may be dangerous yourself.

8 **Fight back if you are attacked.**
Most mountain lions are small enough that an average size human will be able to ward off an attack by fighting back aggressively. Hit the mountain lion in the head, especially around the eyes and mouth. Use your walking stick, fists, or whatever is at hand. Do not curl up and play dead. Mountain lions generally leap down upon prey from above and deliver a "killing bite" to the back of the neck. Their technique is to break the neck and knock down the prey, and they also will rush and lunge up at the neck of prey, dragging the victim down while holding the neck in a crushing grip. Protect your neck and throat at all costs.

HOW TO AVOID AN ATTACK

Mountain lions, also called cougars, have been known to attack people without provocation; aggressive ones have attacked hikers and especially small children, resulting in serious injury. Still, most mountain lions will avoid people. To minimize your contact with cougars in an area inhabited by them, avoid hiking alone and at dusk and dawn, when mountain lions are more active.

PRO TIPS

▶ Though you cannot outrun a cougar, predatory cats in "chasing" attacks tend to focus on deer or other prey that stumble or become disabled on uneven ground. If you are on a road or other flat terrain and not in deep snow or on a rocky incline, running away quickly may show that you are not disabled prey and may be a useful means of escape. This strategy will not be effective for a stealth attack.

▶ Because they are stealth hunters, mountain lions are very effective at following potential prey without being spotted. Turn around regularly while hiking to check the terrain behind you and make sure you are not being tracked.

▶ Mountain lions can climb trees, and may follow small prey up the trunk.

HOW TO WRESTLE FREE FROM AN ALLIGATOR

1 **Hug it.**

If the alligator gets you in its jaws, you must prevent it from shaking you or from rolling over—these instinctual actions cause severe tissue damage. If you are on land (or even in water, though it may be more difficult), try to wrap the body parts not being held around the alligator, as if you are giving it a hug. This will make it more difficult for the alligator to shake or twist. (It will also make it more difficult for the animal to swim or carry you away.) This maneuver may also convince the alligator that its chosen prey is larger than first thought, and encourage it to give up.

2 **Struggle.**

The alligator will be more likely to give up during an attack if it feels it has underestimated the nature of its prey. Struggling will convince it that you are not defenseless.

To get an alligator to release something it has in its mouth, hit it on the snout.

3 **Hit the snout.**

If the alligator's jaws are still closed on something you want to remove (for example, a limb), slap it on the snout: some alligators may open their mouths and drop whatever it is they have taken hold of, and back off.

4 **Go for the eyes and nose.**

If the alligator still has not given up, use any weapon you have, or your fists. Alligators are well adapted to taking down large, strong animals, and are covered with armor-like scaled skin. The eyes and nose are the only soft tissue areas that are vulnerable to attack.

5 **Keep fighting.**

You may notice the alligator sink its eyes down into its head in order to protect them. Jab harder, and add punches and slaps to the eye areas.

6 **Seek medical attention immediately.**

Get medical attention right away, even for a small cut or bruise, to treat infection. Alligators have a huge number of pathogens in their mouths.

HOW TO AVOID AN ATTACK

While deaths in the United States from alligator attacks are rare, there are potentially thousands of attacks and hundreds of fatalities from Nile crocodiles in Africa and saltwater crocodiles in Asia and Australia. Here are a few tips to keep in mind:

▸ Do not swim or wade in areas alligators are known to inhabit (in Florida, this can be anywhere there is fresh or even brackish water). This includes artificial water features on golf courses and water retention ponds in suburban subdivisions.

▸ Do not swim or wade alone, and always check out the area before venturing in.

▸ Do not walk dogs close to fresh water in southern states where alligators are present: dogs have no natural understanding of alligators and may not be wary like a cat.

▸ Do not harass, try to touch, or capture any alligator.

- Do not dangle arms and legs from boats, and avoid throwing unused bait or fish from a boat or dock, particularly at dawn or nighttime, when alligators feed.

- Leave alligator babies and eggs alone. Any adult alligator will respond to a distress call from any youngster.

- Mother alligators guarding nests and babies will defend them vigorously.

- Never feed alligators. In most cases of attack, the alligators had been fed by humans prior to the attack. This is an important link—feeding alligators seems to cause them to lose their fear of humans and become more aggressive. Feeding alligators is also illegal in Florida and other states.

HOW TO ESCAPE FROM KILLER BEES

1 **Run.**

If bees begin flying around and/or stinging you, do not freeze. Run away.

2 **Shield vulnerable areas.**

Cover eyes and nose with your shirt to protect these sensitive areas, but make sure you can still see where you are running. If small children are present, pick them up and take them with you.

3 **Do not swat.**

Bees are attracted to movement, and killed/crushed bees emit a scent that will attract more bees. Swatting at the bees only makes them more aggressive.

4 **Get indoors as fast as you can.**

The bees will follow you indoors, but will become confused by bright lights and windows, and tracking you will become more difficult. Once inside, get under thick blankets and sheets until the bees dissipate.

Run away from killer bees. If no shelter is available, run through bushes or high weeds.

5 **If no shelter is available, run through bushes or high weeds.**

This will help give you cover and make bee navigation more difficult.

6 **If a bee stings you, it will leave its stinger in your skin.**

Remove the stinger by raking your fingernail across it in a sideways motion. Do not pinch or pull the stinger out—this may squeeze more venom from the stinger into your body. Do not let stingers remain in the skin, because venom can continue to pump into the body for up to 10 minutes. Drag a dull knife or credit card across the skin to help remove stingers.

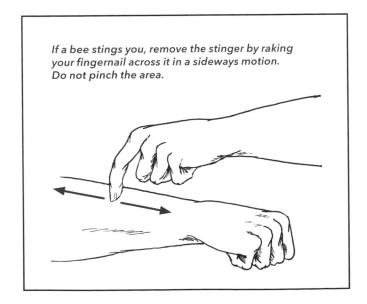

If a bee stings you, remove the stinger by raking your fingernail across it in a sideways motion. Do not pinch the area.

7 **Do not jump into a swimming pool or other body of water.**

The bees are likely to be waiting for you when you surface.

RISK OF ATTACK

▶ The Africanized honeybee is a cousin of the run-of-the-mill domesticated honeybee. The "killer bee" moniker was created after news reports about several deaths that resulted from Africanized bee stings. Africanized honeybees are considered "wild"; they are easily angered by animals and people, and likely to become aggressive.

▶ Bees "swarm" most often in the spring and fall. This is when the entire colony moves to establish a new hive. They may move in large swarms until they find a suitable spot. Once the colony is built and the bees begin raising their young, they will protect their hive by stinging.

▶ While any colony of bees will defend its hive, Africanized bees do so with gusto. These bees can kill, and they present a danger even to those who are not allergic to bee stings. In several isolated instances, people and animals have been stung to death. Regular honeybees will chase you about 50 yards. Africanized honeybees may pursue you three times that distance.

▶ Most often, death from stings occurs when people are not able to get away from the bees quickly. Animal losses have occurred for the same reasons—pets and livestock were tied up or penned when they encountered the bees and could not escape.

HOW TO AVOID AN ATTACK

▶ Avoid colony formation by filling in holes or cracks in exterior walls, filling in tree cavities, and putting screens on the tops of rainspouts and over water meter boxes in the ground.

▶ Do not bother bee colonies: if you see that bees are building—or have already built—a colony around your home, do not disturb them unless they are causing a specific hazard or problem. Call a pest control center to find out who removes bees. If the hive seems to host honeybees, contact a local beekeeper, who may be able to help relocate them.

PRO TIP

A nonallergic person can survive about 10 bee stings per pound of body weight, albeit uncomfortably.

HOW TO DEAL WITH A CHARGING BULL

1   **Do not antagonize the bull, and do not move.**

Bulls will generally leave humans alone unless they become angry.

2   **If it continues charging at you, find a safe haven.**

Running away is not likely to help unless you find an open door, a fence to jump, or another safe haven—bulls can easily outrun humans. If you can reach a safe spot, make a run for it.

3   **Remove your shirt, hat, or another article of clothing.**

If a safe haven is not available, remove an article of clothing to use as a distraction. It does not matter what color the clothing is. Despite the colors bullfighters traditionally use, bulls do not naturally head for red—they react to movement, not color.

4   **Throw your shirt or hat away from you.**

The bull should head toward the object you've thrown.

If you cannot find safe cover from a charging bull, remove articles of clothing and throw them away from your body.

IF YOU ENCOUNTER A STAMPEDE

If you encounter a stampede of bulls or cattle, there will be no way to distract them. Determine which way they're headed and get out of the way. If that isn't possible, your only option is to run alongside the stampede to avoid getting trampled. Bulls are not like horses, and they will not avoid you if you lie down—so keep moving.

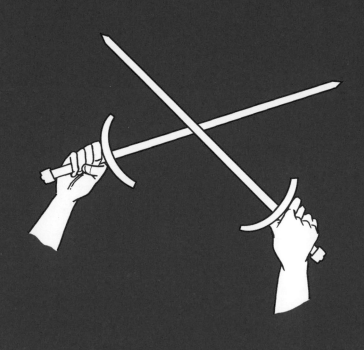

CHAPTER THREE

The Best Defense

HOW TO WIN A SWORD FIGHT

In a fight with an opponent wielding a broad sword or other sharp-edged long blade, your first step is to control their weapon. If it is moving toward you, parry. If it's moving away from you, strike. Remember: blows win sword fights; parries, guards, and steps do not. Defend with the middle part of your sword blade, and attack with the point or the last 10 inches of the cutting edge.

HOW TO PARRY AND STRIKE

1   **If right-handed, keep your sword low and to your left.**
Parry the blow as you move to your right, and beat any attack away to your right, aiming to meet the middle of their blade with the middle of yours. Always parry with the middle of your sword, not the point. Beat the blow away, forcing it away from your body. Don't try to absorb or stop it with your own sword.

2 If a blow is aimed at your head, move your sword so the blade is sloped a bit toward the ground and above your head.

3 Though it may be difficult, always try to move out toward your opponent, even if you are defending.

Cut and thrust using short, quick movements of your sword, not long slashes, which may put you off-balance and open you up to a severe jab.

HOW TO ATTACK

1 Move the sword in quick motions up and down and to the left and right.

Assuming you must disable your attacker, make as many fast, small jabs as you can, with the goal of opening up a series of wounds.

2 Keep the sword in front of you.

Do not raise the blade up behind your head to try a huge blow—you will end up with a sword in your gut.

3 Step into a blow or deflect it to the side.

This may put an untrained opponent off-balance. Once your opponent is off-balance, you can take advantage of their moment of weakness by attacking with your point. A deep penetrating wound may end the fight quickly.

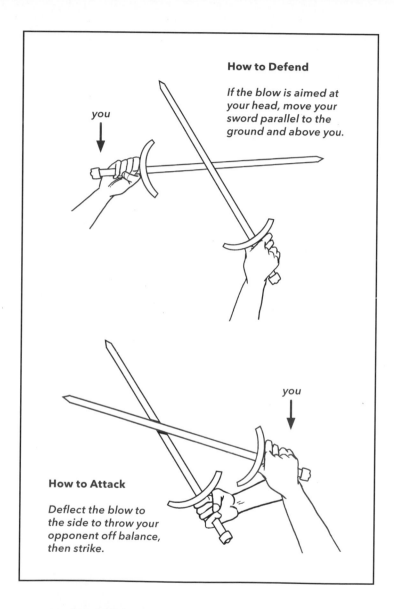

How to Defend

If the blow is aimed at your head, move your sword parallel to the ground and above you.

you

How to Attack

Deflect the blow to the side to throw your opponent off balance, then strike.

you

IF YOU FACE MULTIPLE ATTACKERS

1 **If you are right-handed, move to your right and attack the person on your far right.**

Maneuver this person to keep them in the way of their confederates.

2 **Keep moving and striking, maneuvering to prevent them from getting behind you.**

Keep your back to a wall if possible.

3 **Use strong cuts or slashes.**

In this situation, use cutting and slashing moves, since jabs may result in your sword getting caught in an attacker's clothing, leaving you defenseless against the other opponents.

HOW TO TAKE A PUNCH

BLOW TO THE BODY

1 Tighten your stomach muscles.

A body blow to the gut (solar plexus) can damage organs and kill. This sort of punch is one of the best and easiest

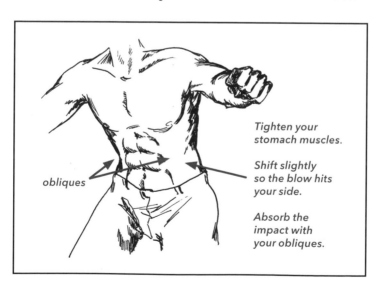

obliques

Tighten your
stomach muscles.

Shift slightly
so the blow hits
your side.

Absorb the
impact with
your obliques.

ways to knock someone out. (Legend has it that Harry Houdini died from an unexpected blow to the abdomen.)

2   **Do not flinch or move away from the punch.**

3   **Shift so that the blow hits your side; move in to reduce its force.**
Try to absorb the blow with your obliques: this is the set of muscles on your side that wraps around your ribs. While a blow to this area may crack a rib, it is less likely to do damage to internal organs.

4   **Absorb the blow with your arm.**
Move your arm into a blocking position to absorb the blow, if you have time.

BLOW TO THE HEAD

1   **Move toward the blow, not away from it.**
Getting punched while moving backward will result in the head taking the punch at full force. A punch to the face can cause head whipping, where the brain moves suddenly inside the skull, and may result in severe injury or death.

2   **Tighten your neck muscles and lower your jaw to your neck.**
This will create a more "unified" object (body, head, and neck).

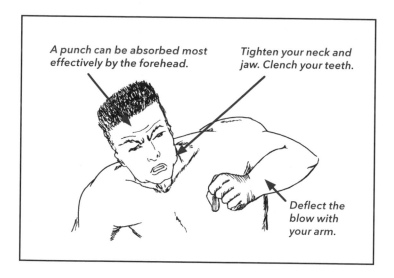

A punch can be absorbed most effectively by the forehead.

Tighten your neck and jaw. Clench your teeth.

Deflect the blow with your arm.

3 **Clench your jaw.**

This will help limit scraping of the upper and lower palettes.

STRAIGHT PUNCH

1 **Move toward the blow.**

The straight punch—one that comes straight at your face—should be countered by moving toward the blow. This will take force from the blow.

2 **Meet the blow with your forehead.**

A punch can be absorbed most effectively and with the least injury by the forehead. Avoid taking the punch in the nose, which is extremely painful.

3 **Attempt to deflect the blow with an arm.**
Moving into the punch may result in your attacker
missing the mark wide to either side.

4 **(Optional) Hit back with an uppercut or roundhouse.**

ROUNDHOUSE

1 **Clench your jaw and tuck your chin.**
A punch to the ear causes great pain and can break your jaw.

2 **Move in close to your attacker.**
Try to make the punch land harmlessly behind your head,
or pass over you. Alternatively, try to roll under the punch.

3 **(Optional) Hit back with an uppercut.**

UPPERCUT

1 **Clench your neck and jaw.**
An uppercut can cause much damage, whipping your
head back, easily breaking your jaw or your nose.

2 **Use your arm to absorb impact or deflect the blow.**
Do anything you can to minimize the impact of a straight
punch to the jaw.

3 **Do not step into this punch.**
Move your head to the side, if possible.

HOW TO FEND OFF A PIRATE ATTACK

GET READY

1 **Watch for the "picket line."**

Smaller fishing boats in close proximity to one another may be a picket line: paid spotters and informers who tip pirates off to potential targets entering their vicinity.

2 **Keep your eyes on the horizon.**

Pirates typically shadow their targets for at least a few days before mounting an attack. Nautical horizon for most ships is about 20 miles. Any vessel within this distance is too close for safety and may be shadowing you.

3 **Monitor your distance from land.**

Friendly naval forces will not attempt to rescue you from a hostile country. Your ship should remain at least a few hundred miles from shore to discourage land-based attacks.

4   **Alert authorities.**

If you suspect an attack is imminent, use your satellite phone to contact the Maritime Security Centre, Horn of Africa (MSCHOA). Report your position and the position of the pirate vessel. Schedule follow-up calls every six hours. A frigate should be dispatched to your location, but must be within about 300 miles, the maximum flying distance of attack helicopters.

5   **Stay awake.**

Pirates typically attack at dawn, when they are most sober.

COUNTER THE ATTACK

1   **Understand pirate tactics.**

Pirates usually operate a main fishing vessel (the mother ship) that tows two "fast-boats": smaller, more maneuverable attack craft. The attack will begin with a direct, high-speed approach by these smaller craft.

2   **Increase speed and zigzag.**

A large ship cannot outrun pirates. Your goal is a series of sharp turns that will create bow waves. These waves may be 10–20 feet high and might capsize the pirate's smaller speedboats.

3   **Deter boarding.**

Pull up the ship's extendible stairway, if present. If it cannot be raised quickly, disconnect it and let it fall into the sea.

4 **Prepare countermeasures.**

Point the ship's firehoses at the pirate ships and turn them on. Stay low. Be prepared to take automatic rifle fire. Your goal is to fill the boats with water and capsize them—or knock attackers overboard.

5 **Use a flare gun to shoot the attacking craft.**

Flares burn at 2000°F and will burn through the pirates' aluminum- or fiberglass-hulled boat in less than a minute, sinking them.

6 **Use broken glass.**

Break empty bottles and scatter the glass on deck; pirates typically go barefoot or wear thin-soled sandals.

7 **Make Molotov cocktails.**

Use the size of your ship, and its height, to your advantage. Fill an empty glass bottle with fuel, insert a rag into the neck, light it, and toss onto pirates below. Repeat as needed. This strategy can be very effective.

8 **Protect the bridge at all costs.**

Snipers on rescue choppers will pick off pirates on the deck at will, but will not attack them once they have breached the bridge. Make sure all doors are closed and locked.

9 **Destroy your passport (unless you're French).**

A passport will allow pirates to quickly identify you and demand ransom from family members; Americans, Brits, and citizens of other wealthy Western nations make appealing targets. Pirates are less likely to kidnap French citizens, due to the French government's steadfast refusal to negotiate—and recent deadly counterattacks by the French military. If you speak French, use it.

PRO TIPS

▸ If you're captured, you (and, most likely, the ship and cargo) will be held for ransom. You will probably be held on the ship, but in rare circumstances may be moved to land.

▸ The pirates will take your identification and pass your information to a land-based accomplice, who will use the Web (and particularly social media) to contact family members or the ship's owner and demand payment. Expect a demand of $50,000 to several million dollars, depending on the value of the ship and its cargo. If you have resisted, you will be beaten.

▸ Ransom payments are typically made, in cash, via airdrop to a specific set of GPS coordinates. To prove you are still alive, the pirates may move you on deck during a flyover. If the money drop goes well, you should be released.

▸ Piracy in the Caribbean Sea is increasingly common and is focused less on kidnapping and more on taking control of U.S.-flagged vessels to be used for transporting contraband. Owners are marooned or, in some cases, killed.

▸ Small vessels have virtually no effective defenses against determined pirates.

HOW TO SURVIVE A HOSTAGE SITUATION

Terrorists need to exercise power and control, and they do this by turning their victims into objects, which are easier to mistreat. Follow these tips to avoid mistreatment or worse.

1 **Stay calm.**

Help others around you to do the same—remember that the hostage takers are extremely nervous and scared. Do not do anything to make them more so. Do not speak to them unless they speak to you.

2 **If shots are fired, keep your head down and drop to the floor.**

Lie flat on your stomach. If you can, get behind a wall, but do not move far—your captors may think that you are attempting to make an escape or an attack. Furniture will not provide sufficient cover, particularly from high-caliber weapons.

3 **Do not make any sudden or suspicious movements.**

Do not attempt to hide your wallet, passport, ticket, or belongings.

4 **Comply with all demands.**

Hesitation on your part may get you killed instantly, or may mark you for later retribution or execution. Remain alert and do not try to escape or be a hero. If you are told to put your hands over your head, to keep your head down, or to get into another body position, do it. It may be uncomfortable, but do not change your position on your own. Talk yourself into relaxing into the position—you may need to stay that way for some time. Prepare both mentally and emotionally for a long ordeal.

5 **Never look at a terrorist directly or raise your head until you are directed to speak to him or her.**

Always raise your hand and address the hostage takers respectfully. When answering questions, be respectful but not submissive. Speak in a regulated tone of voice.

6 **Never challenge a hostage taker.**

They often look for potential execution victims, and if you act contrary in any way, they may select you.

7 **Carefully observe the characteristics and behavior of the terrorists.**

Give them nicknames in your mind so that you can identify them later. Be prepared to describe them by remembering attire, accents, facial characteristics, or height—any aspect that might later help authorities.

8 **If you are the victim of a skyjacking, know where the plane's closest emergency exits are located.**

Count the rows between you and the exit. In the event of an emergency rescue, smoke may obscure visibility, and you must know the fastest path out of the aircraft. Floor or seat LED lighting may guide you if smoke is present. Do not attempt escape unless it is clear that a massacre is imminent.

9 **If a rescue team enters, get down and stay still.**

Shots may be fired, and any sudden movements may draw terrorist or friendly fire.

10 **Upon resolution, be prepared to identify yourself and terrorists to the rescuers.**

Some terrorists may try to exit with you, posing as hostages.

PRO TIPS

- To avoid making yourself attractive to terrorists, try not to take out your passport in public places.

- Be especially alert in airports, train stations, bus stations, lobbies of expensive hotels, and stores that cater to affluent tourists. While civil strife and guerrilla activity usually focus on nationals—thus tourists are relatively safe—terrorists often choose targets that will get them the most attention.

- Promenades, famous landmarks, parade routes, outdoor markets, concerts, and other places where large numbers of people congregate may be targeted by terrorists.

HOW TO SURVIVE A HIJACKING

There are three stages to a hijacking: the Intimidation Phase, the Custodial Phase, and the Resolution Phase (roughly: beginning, middle, and end). The Intimidation Phase, where hijackers assert their authority and attempt to take control, is the most dangerous. In general, your goal is to be a "good" (well-behaved) hostage initially to make it to the middle and end stages without being injured or killed.

1   Listen for an announcement of the hijacking.

An indication of a hijack that is not accompanied by violence is good news. This means the hijackers have a demand or goal they seek to achieve and may not be suicidal.

2   Comply.

If the crew has opted to allow the hijackers to divert the aircraft to their preferred destination, do not do anything to antagonize the hijackers. Do not speak unless spoken to; do not talk back; do not make yourself a target. If the hijackers sense they are losing control, it may lead to "London Syndrome," where a calm situation reverts to the Intimidation Phase and they need to reassert their authority. This situation is especially dangerous, and troublemakers may be singled out for abuse.

3 **Avoid drawing attention to yourself.**

Do not identify yourself as a government employee, or an active member of the military or law enforcement.

4 **Use your phone if possible.**

At low altitude (or on a WiFi-enabled flight) your mobile phone may work. For this reason, the hijackers will probably collect cell phones soon after commandeering the aircraft. If you can do so safely, send an emergency message to alert authorities of the hijacking. If you attempt to hide your phone, the hijackers may not believe you don't have one, and you may be singled out for punishment. At altitude, your phone is unlikely to work over the cellular network.

5 **Assess the hijackers' cause.**

Make a general determination of the hijackers' political views, ultimate goal, or end game. Based on this assessment, if you feel your passport might make you more of a target, conceal it between seats, under your seat cushion, or behind a window shade.

6 **Take advantage of any freedom that is offered.**

If the atmosphere on the plane becomes relatively relaxed, take the opportunity to move around. Use the bathroom. Eat, even if you are not hungry; you don't know when you will have the chance to eat again.

7 **Switch seats quickly.**

Once a hijacking is underway, you are unlikely to have the option of requesting a new seat. However, an aisle seat offers more opportunity for action if you feel you may need to go on the offensive. Move only if it is safe to do so.

8 **Do not assume a sky marshal is present.**

Sky marshals are always seated in aisle seats. However, their presence is highly dependent on the airline. On an Israeli airliner, there will be sky marshals on board. On many other Middle Eastern airlines, as well as those in Asia, sky marshals are likely to be present. In Europe, sky marshals are relatively few in number, and some countries do not deploy them at all. In the United States, there is a chance you might be on a flight with sky marshals on board, but do not count on it.

9 **Observe the cockpit door.**

Since 9/11, regulations require fortified cockpit doors that are difficult to open from the outside. However, the door may be opened occasionally for the pilot or copilot to use the lavatory, or to be served food or beverages by the cabin crew. Hijackers may wait for the door to be opened before trying to take control of the flight deck.

10 **Monitor hijackers' communication with the pilot.**

Airlines train pilots not to open the cockpit door in the event of a hijacking, regardless of threats. Ultimately, however, the pilot is in command and may choose to open the door if he or she feels it is in the best interest of passengers or crew.

11 **Avoid Stockholm, but aim for Lima syndrome.**

In a protracted hijacking, you may become frustrated that the authorities are not doing more to rescue you. Eventually, you may begin to sympathize with the hijackers or their cause—this is known as "Stockholm syndrome." Remember: the hijackers are your enemy. Any delay in rescue is likely for a good reason. Alternatively, during long-duration hijackings focus on working toward "Lima syndrome," where the hijackers start to feel empathy for hostages. Let the hijackers know about you: family, pets, whatever may make them more sympathetic or understanding. (This should be attempted only during the Custodial Phase.)

12 **Listen for shots.**

In the United States, some pilots enroll in the Federal Flight Deck Officer Program, which allows them to carry firearms. As a last resort, they may use their weapon to protect the flight deck. Outside the United States, chances that the pilot (or copilot) is armed are low.

13 **Be ready to attack.**

Most hijackers are not suicidal. However, if there is a shootout—or if you feel the plane may be used as a weapon and a crash seems imminent—you and your fellow passengers have nothing to lose, and must go on the offensive. Use any hard or heavy object available (seat belt buckle, can of soda, oxygen canister) as a makeshift weapon, and coordinate your attack with others nearby. Acting quickly, you may be able to overwhelm a small number of hijackers and retake control.

14 **Comply with security forces.**

If the plane is eventually stormed by SWAT or other armed forces, follow their commands immediately and without hesitation.

PRO TIPS

▶ Sky marshals use frangible ammunition that is designed to explode on impact, not penetrate a target, so the danger of a fuselage penetration from their weapons is low. Hijackers, however, are unlikely to use such ammunition, and any hole from a gunshot may result in decompression of the cabin; a bullet hitting a fuel line or tank could be catastrophic. An explosion, even a small one, may lead to rapid, explosive decompression and loss of the aircraft.

▶ Sky marshals may not react to the hijacking immediately, waiting instead for an opportunity when they believe they have the best chance for success.

HOW TO IDENTIFY
A BOMB

Letter and package bombs can be very dangerous and destructive. However, unlike a bomb that goes off suddenly and with no warning, they can be identified. High-risk search teams keep the following phrase in mind at all times: *Look for the presence of the unusual or the absence of the usual.* Observe the following procedures and warning signs.

HOW TO DETECT A PACKAGE BOMB

1   Examine unexpected parcels or letters.

If a carrier delivers an unexpected bulky letter or parcel, inspect it for lumps, bulges, or protrusions, without applying pressure. Check for unevenly balanced parcels.

2   Note unusual labeling.

Handwritten addresses or labels from companies are unusual. Check to see if the company exists and if they sent a package or letter.

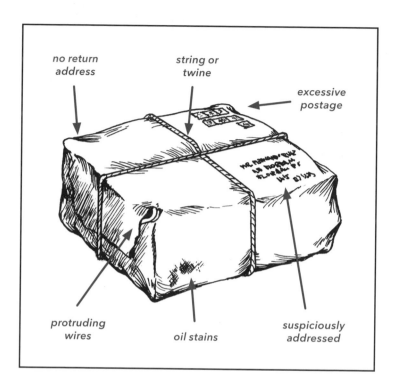

no return
address

string or
twine

excessive
postage

protruding
wires

oil stains

suspiciously
addressed

3 **Be suspicious of packages wrapped in string.**

Modern packaging materials have eliminated the need
for twine or string.

4 **Beware of excessive postage.**

Watch out for excess postage on small packages or
letters—this indicates that the object was not weighed
by the post office. It is no longer legal to mail stamped
parcels weighing more than 16 ounces at mailboxes in the
United States—they must be taken to a post office.

5 **Beware of leaks, stains, protruding wires, or excessive tape.**

Be especially wary of oil stains.

6 **Beware of articles with no return address or a nonsensical return address.**

HOW TO SEARCH FOR A BOMB

Government agencies use well-defined search procedures for bombs and explosive devices. After a bomb threat, the following can be used as a guide for searching a room, using a two-person search team.

1 **Divide the area and select a search height.**

The first searching sweep should cover all items resting on the floor up to the height of furniture; subsequent sweeps should move up from there.

2 **Start back-to-back and work around the room.**

Face in opposite directions, moving toward each other.

3 **Begin searching around the walls.**

Proceed inward in concentric circles toward the center of the room.

4 **If you find a suspicious parcel or device, do not touch it.**

Call emergency services or the bomb squad.

DETECTION DEVICES

There are several types of devices and methods that can be used to identify bombs, including metal and vapor detectors, as well as X-ray machines. Several devices are portable and inexpensive enough for an individual to obtain.

Particulate Explosives Detector

▶ Detects modern plastic explosive constituents as well as TNT and nitroglycerin.

▶ Detects RDX (used in C4, PE4, SX2, Semtex, Demex, and Detasheet), PETN (used in certain military explosives and Semtex), TNT (trinitrotoluene), and NG (nitroglycerin).

▶ Uses IMS (ion mobility spectroscopy) to detect micron-size particles used in explosives. A sample size of one nanogram is sufficient for detection.

▶ To use, swipe the suspect material with a sample wipe or a cotton glove. Analysis time is approximately three seconds. A visual display contains a red warning light and an LCD, giving a graphic display with a relative numerical scale of the target materials identified. An audible alarm can be triggered based on a user-defined threshold.

▶ Requires AC or a battery.

▶ Approximately 15 × 12 × 5 inches.

Portable X-Ray System

- Uses a digital image processor to create detailed images of parcels and packages.

- Requires AC or a rechargeable battery.

- To use, simply point the X-ray generator at the suspect item and view the digital image.

Bomb-Detection Dog

- Specially trained canines are able to detect various types of explosives using their highly attuned sense of smell.

- Walk the dog through the security line at the airport and allow it to sniff carry-on bags.

PRO TIP

All bomb experts stress that avoidance is the key concept when dealing with explosives. Your best chance of survival lies with the bomb squad, not with one of these devices.

HOW TO SURVIVE A PROTEST

PEACEFUL

1 **Dress appropriately.**

Wear comfortable shoes and loose-fitting clothing (in layers, if conditions dictate). Carry or wear a hat and sunscreen in hot weather, and gloves and a warm hat in colder conditions. Avoid dressing in all black: you may be mistaken for an Antifa protester and singled out for abuse. Do not cover your face.

2 **Stay hydrated.**

Carry a backpack with a water reservoir to keep your hands free. In colder conditions, carry a double-walled insulated bottle with coffee, tea, or hot cocoa.

3 **Eat.**

Bring foods appropriate for camping, such as energy/granola bars, dried fruits and nuts, and cured meats that do not require refrigeration.

4 **Stay connected.**

Make sure someone knows you are attending the protest and when you expect to return. Livestreaming or regularly posting on social media will spread your message and let others know you're okay (or in danger).

5 **March on the perimeter.**

When practical, stay on the outer edges of the crowd or march to access escape routes should the protest turn ugly. Note, however, that in this location you may also be the target of direct taunts or threats from counterprotesters.

6 **Keep children close at hand.**

Small children especially should always be in front of you.

7 **Chant, but don't scream.**

Screaming loudly will only make you hoarse and, eventually, cause you to lose your voice. Rest your vocal cords for 15 minutes each hour. Drink honey dissolved in warm water if your throat feels dry, or warm water and lemon if you're phlegmy.

PRO TIP

Carry a portable battery to keep your cell phone charged.

NOT PEACEFUL

1   **Dress in muted tones.**

Bright colors and unusual attire may draw the eye and make you a target.

2   **Check your shoes.**

Your shoes should be secured tightly so they don't come off. Losing your footwear will impact your ability to move quickly to escape the mob.

3   **Scan the crowd and look for openings and exits.**

Try to plot where you want to be located three to four seconds in the future, not the one to two seconds that is common for those desperately seeking to escape a riot. Look for gaps or holes in the mob that are in the general direction of exits or escape routes—as long as they are not at the center of the rioting.

4   **Do not run.**

Unless your life is in imminent danger, walk. Walking is harder for the eye to detect: The human eye can quickly sight someone running. Running can also generate excitement or false hope—people may chase or follow you.

5   **Protect your rib cage.**

Cross your arms in front of your upper body to shield it from being compressed by the crowd. The main cause of death during crushes is an inability to expand the lungs due to pressure from the crowd.

6 **Leave as a group.**

Especially if you have to dash across an open area, such as the front of a building, a wide street, or a plaza, you are safer with company and less likely to be singled out from the herd.

7 **Move away from violent activity or mobs.**

You risk being trampled by rioters if you get too close to the center of violent clashes.

8 **Avoid bottlenecks and "funnels."**

Stampedes of people running toward narrow exits (gates, doorways, alleys) may result in mass casualties as rioters are trampled. However, moving against the crowd is generally not advisable, and may be impossible in any case. To escape, move with the crowd's general direction of travel, but at an angle that will bring you to the edge of the mob and toward an exit.

HOW TO DE-ESCALATE A CONFRONTATION

1 **Ignore angry words.**

These mean nothing, and trying to process them will only provoke your own emotional response.

2 **Gauge the individual's emotional data fields in the moment.**

You may sense anger, hostility, fear, pride, and many other feelings all at once.

3 **Reflect the individual's emotions with "You" statements.**

In a calm voice, say, "You are feeling angry. You are frustrated. You feel disrespected and insulted." Do not use "I" statements, which will only serve to escalate the situation. Do not ask questions.

4 **Monitor verbal and visual cues.**

Wait until the individual:

- ▸ Nods his or her head affirmatively
- ▸ Utters something like, "Exactly"
- ▸ Drops his or her shoulders
- ▸ Sighs

These are unconscious indicators that the protester's emotional centers have quieted down, and a productive dialogue may now be possible.

PRO TIP

All human brains are hard-wired to receive this information, and all human brains crave this level of emotional validation.

HOW TO SURVIVE
BEING TEARGASSED

1   **Quickly survey your surroundings.**

When tear gas is released, it mixes into the air and fills up available space with a toxic cloud. If you suspect tear gas may be deployed, memorize as much of your surroundings as possible, including the locations of nearby exit routes like open streets. Mentally note the location of fixed obstacles including parked cars, streetlights, and crowd-control barriers. Do this to make navigation and escape easier once you've been temporarily blinded by the gas.

2   **Stay calm.**

You may be temporarily blinded, but it is unlikely that you will suffer serious or permanent injury from the gas itself. You are more likely to be injured by dangerous collisions with panicked protesters or fixed obstacles (or authorities).

3   **Protect your face and airway.**

Immediately close your eyes and cover your nose and eyes with your shirt, a cloth hat, a bag, or your hands. (Wear a handkerchief or scarf to the protest to be prepared.)

4   **Move.**

Locate the nearest exit route or open area that has not been hit. The gas will be carried by prevailing winds, so avoid running downwind. Run upwind or laterally to escape clouds of gas, moving to higher elevation if possible. The effects of tear gas can linger in the air for hours or even days.

5 **Keep your eyes closed.**

Resist the temptation to open your eyes until you have clear, cool water available to rinse them. Once away from the gas, move protective clothing (or hands) away from your face to reduce continued exposure to the gas that may have collected.

6 **Rinse your face and airway with clean water.**

Presoaking a bandana or scarf with lemon juice or Coca-Cola is often recommended to reduce the pain of tear gas exposure. However, rinsing the eyes and airway with clean water is the best solution to clear the chemical from your face. After exposure, get rid of or wash any clothing that has been in contact with tear gas.

PRO TIPS

▶ Despite its name, tear gas is not a true gas. The chemicals are solids and typically dispersed within a thick fog. The chemicals trigger tearing, but even exposure to small amounts of tear gas can cause other discomfort: burning eyes, pain in your nose, nausea, chest tightness, shortness of breath, stomach ache, and diarrhea.

▶ A solution of liquid Maalox—mixed 50-50 with water in a spray bottle—sprayed into the eyes and mouth (and swallowed) may reduce the effects of tear gas.

HOW TO SURVIVE A NIGHT IN JAIL

1   **Don't panic or show fear.**

Stand straight and tall, and look straight ahead. Do not attempt to stare down or intimidate other prisoners as you enter the facility. These actions may make you a target for harassment by other prisoners seeking to prove themselves by challenging you.

2   **Avoid provoking other inmates.**

If you are attacked, defend yourself. But do not start a fight just to appear tough, which may result in a longer stay or a move to a higher-security facility.

3   **Mind your own business.**

Nobody in prison is your friend. Speak sparingly or not at all, and do not reveal anything about yourself or your circumstances.

4   **Do not proclaim your innocence.**

Nobody cares, and everyone is innocent.

5   **Steer clear of corrections officers.**

Prisoners, not guards, runs prisons. Guards in privately run jails or prisons may have little experience or may be in business with inmates. Do not assume guards are there to help you. Call for a guard's help only if you feel you are in imminent danger.

6   **Do not make weapons.**

If you are found with a weapon, you will be moved to higher security. Other inmates may also try to curry favor with guards by reporting you if they see a weapon.

7   **Do not join a gang.**

Gang members may be present in some state prisons and local jails. Do not seek out a gang affiliation, and under no circumstances pretend you are already in a gang by using clothing or other visual cues or displays. Such actions will immediately make you a target for other rival gangs.

8   **Do not pay for protection.**

This will be the start of a never-ending cycle of being in debt to other inmates.

9   **Request protective custody.**

If you feel you are in imminent danger, you have the option of asking for protective custody. This will isolate you from other prisoners. However, your request may not be granted.

How to Survive a Longer Sentence

In addition to the preceding advice, you will need to take additional steps to prepare for an extended term in prison.

1 **Prepare finances.**

Most prisons do not allow any business to be conducted over the phone, including financial discussions. You and your family should have a strategy to deal with loss of income.

2 **Prepare children.**

Any child over age four should be told that mommy/daddy did something wrong and is going to be away for a year or two. (The child will find out during visitations anyway.)

3 **Prepare yourself.**

You may not be guilty, but you have been found guilty. Accept that prison is your fate, and concentrate on improving yourself, helping other inmates, and avoiding boredom.

4 **Fund your commissary account.**

In U.S. federal prison, your account may hold a maximum of $300 per month in credit; most inmates' families do not have the resources to fully fund their accounts. You will visit the commissary once per week, where you must purchase essentials (soap, toothpaste) and may buy snacks, a radio, and other items. Some commissary purchases have high trade value among inmates, particularly packets of tuna and mackerel. Items in the commissary are priced similarly to what you will find on the outside.

5 **Stay out of trouble.**

In addition to keeping you from being sent to a harsher institution, good behavior earns "good time," which can shave months or years from your sentence. Rates vary with institutions, but federal and many state prisons offer 53-day reductions for each year of good time served.

6 **Get a job.**

Prison jobs in the United States can average $3.45 per hour (but can also pay much lower). This money goes into your commissary account. The real value of such jobs can be reducing boredom. Except in rural southern states, prison jobs do not include hard labor or chain-gang-style road work; most support the institution. Consider a laundry, landscaping, or carpentry job.

7 **Help other inmates.**

The best way to do easy time in prison is to be a valued prisoner. Use your particular skill set and education to help others improve: teach a GED class (or equivalent that shows learning proficiency), lead a book discussion group, help prepare appeal briefs, and so on. Prison staff will also appreciate your contributions.

HOW TO SURVIVE IF YOU ARE IN THE LINE OF GUNFIRE

IF YOU ARE THE PRIMARY TARGET

1 **Get as far away as possible.**

An untrained shooter isn't likely to be accurate at any distance greater than 60 feet.

2 **Run fast, but do not move in a straight line.**

Run in unpredictable/unrhythmic zigzags, which will make it difficult for the shooter to draw a bead on you. The average shooter will not have the training necessary to hit a moving target at any real distance.

3 **Do not bother to count shots.**

You will have no idea if the shooter has more ammunition. Counting is only for the movies. However, any glimpse at the weapon and remembered detail may provide crucial information to authorities once you escape.

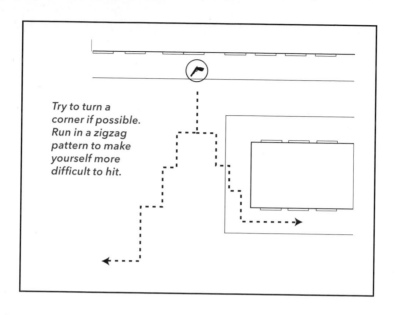

Try to turn a corner if possible. Run in a zigzag pattern to make yourself more difficult to hit.

4 **Turn a corner as quickly as you can, particularly if your pursuer has a rifle or assault weapon.**

Rifles have much greater accuracy and range, and the person may be more likely to either aim or spray bullets in your direction.

5 **Once behind the corner, continue to stay low.**

Untrained shooters tend to shoot at shoulder/chest height. If you stay low, such shots should go above you. If the shooter aims low, it is likely he will miss and hit the ground.

6 **Do not overestimate your cover.**

Even a brick wall may not stop high-caliber assault rifle ammunition.

IF YOU ARE NOT THE PRIMARY TARGET

It is very likely that you'll hear gunfire before you see it. Resist the temptation to run aimlessly; assess the situation first.

1 **Get down and stay down.**

If the intended target is near you or if the shooter is firing at random, get as low as possible. Do not crouch down; get flat on your stomach and stay there.

2 **If you are outside and can get to a car, run to it.**

Lie behind a tire on the opposite side of the car from the shooter. If no cars are present, lie in the gutter next to the

Try to keep large objects between you and the shooter.

curb. A car may stop or deflect a small-caliber bullet fired toward you. However, higher caliber bullets—such as those from an assault rifle or bullets that are designed to pierce armor—can easily penetrate a car and hit someone on the opposite side.

3 **If you are inside a building and the shooter is inside, get to another room and lie flat.**

If you cannot get to another room, move behind any heavy, thick objects (a solid desk, filing cabinets, tables, a couch) for protection.

4 **If you are face-to-face with the shooter, do anything you can to make yourself less of a target.**

Turn sideways, and stay low—stray bullets are likely to be at least a few feet above the ground. If the shooter is outside, stay inside and stay away from doors and windows.

5 **Stay down until the shooting stops or until authorities arrive and give the all clear.**

PRO TIP

The shooter is under significant stress, and any fired and missed shot is a saved life. Raise the probability of the shooter missing you by:

▸ Being out of sight

▸ Being a small target

▸ Not drawing attention

HOW TO TELL IF SOMEONE IS LYING TO YOU

Use the following vocal and visual cues to determine if someone may be lying to you.

- **Their pitch is high.**
  The pitch of the speaker's voice is high from a stress tightening of the vocal cords.

- **The person employs *shielding*.**
  They cover their mouth or eyes with their hand while speaking.

- **They pause.**
  In response to a question, there is a long pause or delay before an answer is offered.

- **They complain.**
  The person complains often and/or makes lots of negative statements.

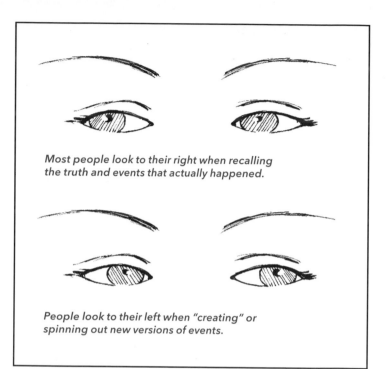

Most people look to their right when recalling the truth and events that actually happened.

People look to their left when "creating" or spinning out new versions of events.

- **They are ill at ease.**

  The speaker seems generally ambivalent, nervous, tense, or ill at ease, including in their body language.

- **What they are saying sounds "fishy."**

  Their story may sound generally implausible to an objective observer.

- **They avoid detail.**

  The information given is lacking in detail.

- **They are inconsistent.**

  The speaker's story has inconsistencies. The person's general communication and demeanor may also be inconsistent. For example, the facial expression or tone of voice may not match the emotions in their words.

  PRO TIP

  These and related actions may convey the speaker's anxiety, which is not necessarily (or always) a sign of untruths. For example, excessive perspiration may indicate that the speaker is nervous, but not knowingly lying to you.

HOW TO TELL IF YOU ARE BEING GASLIGHTED

Gaslighting is a tactic of psychological manipulation and deception used to exert power and ego over those on the receiving end, with the aim to make them question their own reality, or even sanity.

1 Determine intent.

Everyone becomes defensive from time to time, dodging or "correcting" challenges to their beliefs—especially in emotionally charged situations. Absolute gaslighters will stop at nothing to obtain self-gratifying validation. Determining whether you are facing everyday defensiveness or absolute authoritarianism will help you handle your response to the situation.

2 **Concede that the potential gaslighter could be right, and see if it softens their tone.**

Offer, "I could be wrong, but this is what I have learned/heard/read." If the potential gaslighter is conciliatory ("I agree—I could be wrong, too.") then you are probably just dealing with everyday defensiveness. If met with a more autocratic tone ("Yes—you ARE wrong.") then you are likely dealing with an absolute gaslighter.

3 **If you are being skirted, deflected, and corrected at every turn, assume that you are dealing with an absolute gaslighter.**

Gaslighters are formulaic in their rebuttals, and will never concede that you have any chance of being correct. They will "nope" and gloat relentlessly, and perceive themselves as infallible, invincible, and unassailable.

4 **Attempt to change the subject or leave the conversation.**

If you can sidestep a gaslighter, do so. You will never convince them of your side of the argument or of your beliefs.

5 **Challenge the gaslighter on the basis of their broader approach, rather than on the particulars.**

Ask the gaslighter why they are "always defensive." Being confronted on their wall-to-wall defensiveness will be met with more defensiveness, proving your point. Be tenacious. Avoid particulars. Say "there you go again," exposing their one trick again and again.

6 **Admit your own fallibility, even if the gaslighter will not.**

A gaslighter will police you on your every response to their purported infallibility. This will likely include insulting your intelligence, your beliefs, or your self. Do not bother to defend yourself, as doing so will cede the power dynamic to the gaslighter by playing their game. Instead, admit proudly to your human fallibility and shame them for pretending that they are infallible. "We are all occasionally name-callers, or hypocrites, or incorrect in our beliefs—I am simply able to acknowledge that. You seem unable to do so."

7 **Agree to disagree.**

You will never win an argument with a gaslighter—just stay true to your own values and beliefs, and let the conflict subside. Disengage from the situation as soon as possible.

HOW TO TELL IF A CLOWN IS MURDEROUS

1 **Do not immediately assume that a clown is dangerous.**

Although many people feel that clowns are inherently creepy, not all clowns are serial killers, supernatural creatures, or demons in clown attire. Most clowns you are likely to encounter are simply street performers, are heading to a circus or birthday party, or are simply seeking gainful employment.

2 **Look for clues as to the clown's intentions.**

From a safe distance, try to determine whether or not the clown is safe or dangerous.

▶ Does the clown have a hat or valise on the sidewalk full of tips and coins?

Likelihood: **SAFE**

▶ Does the clown carry humorous props and gifts, such as squirting flowers or balloon animals?

Likelihood: **SAFE**

- ▶ Did the clown emerge from a small vehicle with multiple other clowns of various types?

Likelihood: **SAFE**

- ▶ Is the clown on the street in broad daylight?

Likelihood: **SAFE**

- ▶ Is the clown hiding in the woods, bushes, or a sewer drain?

Likelihood: **DANGEROUS**

- ▶ Does the clown carry weapons of a non-humorous nature, such as a baseball bat, a butcher knife, or an axe?

Likelihood: **DANGEROUS**

- ▶ Does the clown have sharp teeth?

Likelihood: **DANGEROUS**

- ▶ Does the clown have creepy eyes?

Likelihood: **DANGEROUS**

- ▶ Does the clown appear to have blood on his/her costume?

Likelihood: **DANGEROUS**

3 **Do not accept gifts from strange looking clowns.**
Dangerous clowns often use colorful lollipops, balloons, stuffed animals, or dolls to make themselves appear friendly. Only accept gifts from clowns in public areas such as circuses, street fairs, and birthday parties, and only if there is empirical evidence that such gifts are safe (i.e., others have accepted them and are using them).

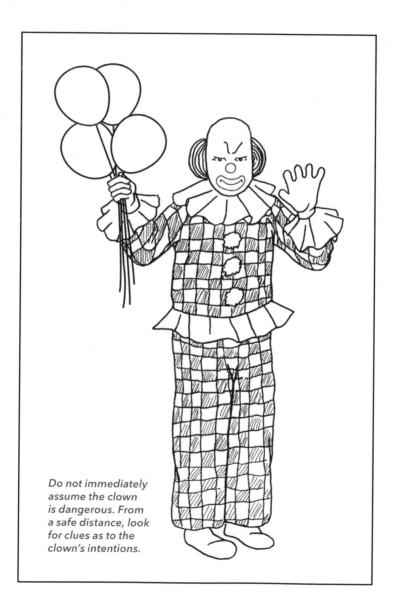

Do not immediately assume the clown is dangerous. From a safe distance, look for clues as to the clown's intentions.

4   **Never get into a vehicle or an enclosed drainpipe with a clown.**

Real clowns provide entertainment, not transportation or subterranean infrastructural education.

PRO TIP

The intense fear of clowns is known as *coulrophobia*. While not recognized as an official diagnosis or disorder by the American Psychiatric Association, those who experience the condition may suffer a range of symptoms, including panic, nausea, and shortness of breath. Psychologists point to a number of possible factors that can drive such fear, including paint masks distorting facial features and expressions, and the expectation that clowns are playful and even manic, and therefore unpredictable.

CHAPTER FOUR

Leaps of Faith

HOW TO JUMP FROM A BRIDGE OR CLIFF INTO A RIVER

When attempting an emergency high fall of 20 feet or more into water, you are not likely to know the depth of the water. This makes jumping particularly dangerous.

If jumping from a bridge into a river or other body of water with boat traffic, try to land in the channel—the deep water generally toward the center, where boats go under the bridge. Do not jump near the bridge's support pylons, which can collect debris and present an additional danger.

1   **Jump feet first.**

2   **Keep your body completely vertical.**

3   **Squeeze your feet together.**
Clench your teeth and keep your head in a neutral position.

4   **Enter the water feet first, and clench your buttocks together.**
If you do not, water may rush in and cause severe internal damage.

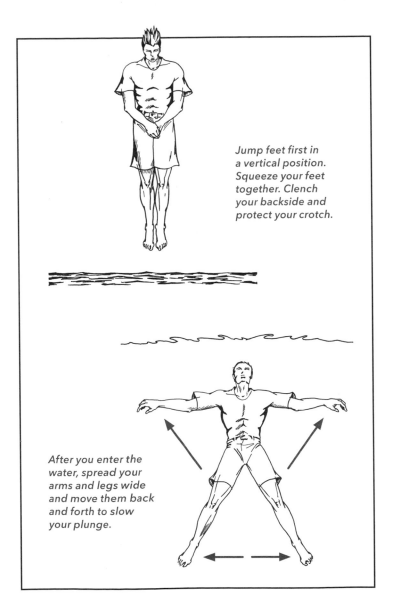

Jump feet first in a vertical position. Squeeze your feet together. Clench your backside and protect your crotch.

After you enter the water, spread your arms and legs wide and move them back and forth to slow your plunge.

5   Protect your crotch area by covering it with your hands.

6   Immediately after you hit the water, spread your arms and legs wide.

Move them back and forth to generate resistance and slow your plunge. Always assume the water is not deep enough to keep you from hitting bottom.

7   Swim to shore immediately after surfacing.

PRO TIPS

▸ Hitting the water this way could save your life, although it may break your legs.

▸ If your body is not straight, you can break your back upon entry. Do not flail arms. Keep yourself vertical until you hit the water.

▸ Do not even think about going in headfirst unless you are absolutely sure that the water is at least 20 feet deep. If your legs hit the bottom, they will break. If your head hits, your skull will break.

▸ When done correctly, a jump from a height of up to 170 feet is survivable.

HOW TO JUMP FROM A BUILDING INTO A DUMPSTER

1 **Jump straight down.**

If you leap off and away from the building at an angle, your trajectory will make you miss the dumpster. Resist your natural tendency to push off.

2 **Tuck your head and bring your legs around.**

To do this during the fall, execute a three-quarter revolution—a not-quite-full somersault. This is the only method that will allow a proper landing, with your back facing down.

3 **Aim for the center of the dumpster or large box of debris.**

4 **Land flat on your back so that when your body folds, your feet and hands meet.**

When your body hits any surface from a significant height, the body folds into a V. This means landing on your stomach can result in a broken back.

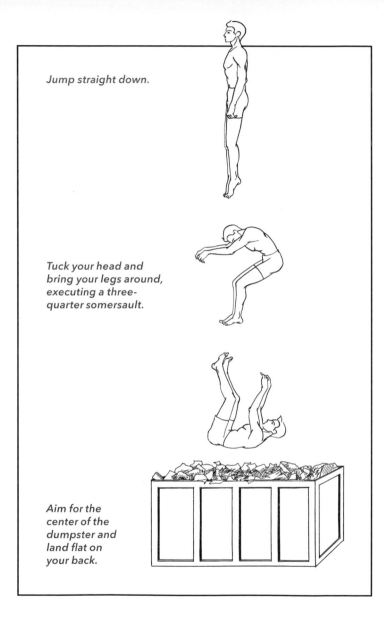

Jump straight down.

Tuck your head and bring your legs around, executing a three-quarter somersault.

Aim for the center of the dumpster and land flat on your back.

PRO TIPS

▶ If the building has fire escapes or other protrusions, your leap will have to be far enough out so you miss them on your way down. The landing target needs to be far enough from the building for you to hit it.

▶ The dumpster may be filled with bricks or other unfriendly materials. It is entirely possible to survive a high fall (five stories or more) into a dumpster, provided it is filled with the right type of trash (cardboard boxes are best) and you land correctly.

HOW TO MANEUVER ON TOP OF A MOVING TRAIN AND GET INSIDE

1 Do not try to stand up straight (you probably will not be able to anyway).

Stay bent slightly forward, leaning into the wind. If the train is moving faster than 30 miles per hour, it will be difficult to maintain your balance and resist the wind, so crawling on all fours may be the best method until you can get down.

2 If the train is approaching a turn, lie flat; do not try to keep your footing.

The car may have guide rails along the edge to direct water. If it does, grab them and hold on.

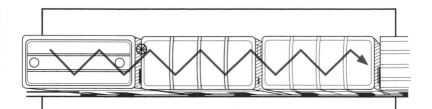

*Crouch low and move slowly forward,
swaying with the side-to-side motion of the train.
Look for a ladder between cars.*

3 **If the train is approaching a tunnel entrance, lie flat quickly.**

There is actually quite a bit of clearance between the top of the train and the top of the tunnel—about three feet—but not nearly enough room to stand. Do not assume that you can walk or crawl to the end of the car to get down and inside before you reach the tunnel—you probably won't.

4 **Move your body with the rhythm of the train—from side to side and forward.**

Do not proceed in a straight line. Spread your feet apart about 36 inches and wobble from side to side as you move forward.

5 **Find the ladder at the end of the car (between two cars) and climb down.**

Due to tight tunnel clearances, it is very unlikely that there will be a ladder on the side of the car—they usually appear only in the movies, to make the stunts more exciting.

PRO TIPS

▶ The sizes and shapes of the cars on a freight train may vary widely. This can either make it easier or significantly more difficult to cross from one car to another.

▶ A 12-foot-high boxcar may be next to a flatbed or a rounded chem car. If on this type of train, your best bet is to get down as quickly as possible, rather than to try a dangerous leap from car to car.

▶ With exceptions for some commuter railroads, railcars on modern passenger trains are now joined with accordion-style connectors, making climbing inside from the end of the car impossible. In this situation, you will need to walk to the front (or rear, if a trailing locomotive is present) and climb down between a passenger car and the locomotive.

HOW TO JUMP FROM A MOVING CAR

Hurling yourself from a moving car should be a last resort—for example if your brakes are defective and your car is about to head off a cliff or into a train.

1 **Apply the emergency brake.**

This may not stop the car, but it might slow it down enough to make jumping safer.

2 **Open the car door.**

3 **Make sure you jump at an angle that will take you out of the path of the car.**

Since your body will be moving at the same velocity as the car, you're going to continue to move in the direction the car is moving. If the car is going straight, try to jump at an angle that will take you away from it.

4 **Tuck in your head and your arms and legs.**

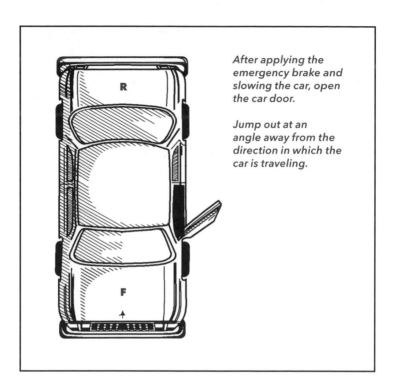

After applying the emergency brake and slowing the car, open the car door.

Jump out at an angle away from the direction in which the car is traveling.

5 **Aim for a soft landing site: grass, brush, wood chips, anything but pavement or a tree.**

Stuntpeople wear pads and land in sandpits. You won't have this luxury, but anything that gives a bit when the body hits it will minimize injury.

6 **Roll when you hit the ground.**

Try to land on your shoulder, and then logroll perpendicular to the direction of travel. Do not try to roll in a somersault.

HOW TO LEAP FROM A MOTOR-CYCLE INTO A CAR

1 **Survey the road ahead.**

Traffic should be clear, with no cars that may be overtaken. The maneuver should be attempted only on a straightaway: turns or sudden lane changes may cause the bike and car to separate.

2 **Match speed of the target vehicle.**

The bike and the car should be traveling at the same speed.

3 **Approach the front passenger side window.**

Do not attempt to leap into the rear seat, on either side of the car. The rear window opening is a smaller target, and the C pillar is difficult to grab. Make sure the window is rolled down all the way.

4 **Prepare to leap.**

Get as close as possible. Keep your left (car-side) foot on the foot peg, while you carefully move your right foot up onto the motorcycle seat. Maintain your grip on the handlebars. Keep weight on left foot.

Leap into the front passenger window.

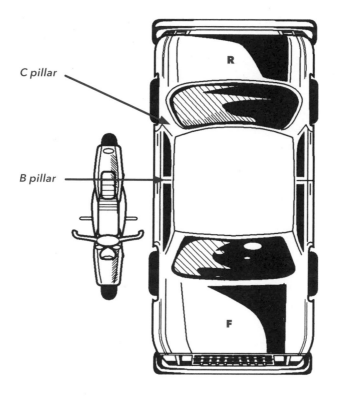

C pillar

B pillar

R

F

*Make sure the window is rolled down
all the way, and move at the same speed
as the car. Get as close as possible.*

5   **Push off using your left leg only.**

Pushing with your right leg may cause the bike to tip or slide out from under you.

6   **Aim for the open window and jump.**

Keep arms outstretched. The bike should stay upright for at least several seconds as it slows and then crashes.

7   **If you miss the window, grab for the B pillar.**

The B pillar is welded to the car frame and is one of the strongest areas of the chassis. If you miss the window, grab the B post and hold on tightly. Swing one leg and then the other through the front window. Or ask the driver to lower the rear window and climb in the back.

8   **If you miss the B pillar, tuck and roll.**

If you miss both the window and the B pillar, tuck and roll your body away from the vehicles.

PRO TIPS

▸   The move is much easier if two people are on the motorcycle so that the non-jumper can continue driving.

▸   In movies, these transfers are usually done at slow speeds and often employ a metal step installed on one side of the bike or car, allowing the rider to step off while keeping the bike balanced. You are not likely to have this option.

HOW TO JUMP FROM ONE CAR INTO ANOTHER

1 **Monitor speed and distance.**

The faster the cars are moving, the greater the wind resistance acting on the jumper and the closer the cars need to be. At any speed greater than 50 miles per hour, they should be even.

2 **Check the lead vehicle.**

If possible, attempt your jump into a convertible (with the top down), which offers a larger and more forgiving target. A pickup truck is another good option.

3 **Move to the rear seat and open the window.**

4 **Align the two vehicles.**

The chase car should approach the lead car from its passenger side, targeting the front passenger window.

5 **Maintain speed.**

6 **Crawl through the window.**

Hold onto the roof with one hand and the B pillar with the other.

7 **Position your legs and feet.**

Keep your left leg outside the car while you place your right foot on the windowsill.

8 **Jump.**

With right leg bent, push off the windowsill, keeping your arm out ahead of you. Go headfirst into the lead car's front passenger window. If the lead car is a convertible or pickup, aim for the backseat or truck bed.

9 **If you miss, grab for the B pillar, or tuck and roll.**

If you miss, grab the B pillar and pull yourself in. If you miss the B pillar, tuck your body in and roll away from the vehicles.

CHAPTER FIVE

Technical Trouble

HOW TO SURVIVE A FLAMING CELL PHONE

1 **Act fast.**

The phone (or other device containing a lithium ion battery) may catch fire suddenly and with little or no warning. Because the fire is precipitated by a chemical reaction, the phone may combust when powered on or off. As soon as the phone begins to feel warm, you will have just seconds to act.

2 **Remove pants.**

If the phone is in your pocket, do not attempt to grab it. Instead, take your pants off. If the phone is in a handbag, be ready to fling the bag away from you and others nearby.

3 **Do not attempt to save the phone.**

Once the chemical reaction in the battery begins to go haywire, the phone's internal circuitry will be damaged and the device will be lost. Do not attempt to power it down. Do not try to hold the phone and call for help: the call may not go through, and you may be injured.

4 **Do not smother.**

Any battery that uses an oxidation/reduction reaction to generate energy does not require a supply of external oxygen. Do not attempt to cut off oxygen by smothering the fire—this will not be effective, and may result in burns.

5 **Avoid inhaling smoke.**

Phones are filled with metals and plastics that will emit irritating and potentially toxic smoke when burned.

6 **Locate suitable body of water.**

The safest way to prevent the fire from spreading is to submerge the phone in water. If near a beach or lake, quickly toss the phone into shallow water. If at home, toss it in the toilet. If at a restaurant, grab an ice bucket. If no water is present, toss the phone to the ground, away from combustible materials, and allow it to burn itself out.

7 **Wait 10 minutes.**

Small devices like phones will not burn for very long, but may remain warm to the touch for several minutes after the fire goes out. Make sure the phone is completely cool before handling.

PRO TIP

Very hot conditions may exacerbate the defects that lead to a phone fire. Do not leave your phone in a hot car or in direct sunlight on a hot day.

HOW TO SURVIVE DROPPING A CELL PHONE IN THE TOILET

1   **Get the phone out of the toilet ASAP.**

The longer it's submerged, the greater the chance of water damage is going to be.

2   **Turn off the phone immediately.**

When water meets electronics, a short circuit is the surest cause of irreparable damage.

3   **Take off the case.**

If you have one, remove any protective case and/or screen shield. Place these accessories on paper towels to dry out.

4   **Shake it out.**

Vigorously shake the phone up and down, removing all excess droplets.

5 **Remove as many components as possible.**

Unplug any headphones, and remove the SIM card. If possible, open the back cover and remove the battery. Dry all removable components thoroughly with tissue or paper towels.

6 **Clean the phone.**

Using a clean cloth towel, gently blot the USB slot, the headphone jack, and other open-air areas of the phone. Be careful not to push any water further inside the phone in the process.

7 **Stick the phone in a container of drying agent.**

Find a container with a lid and fill it with a drying agent—experts recommend silica gel ("crystal" cat litter) or couscous. Place the phone, battery, and SIM card inside, completely covering them. Make sure the phone is positioned vertically, so any residual water can drain out the bottom. Then seal the lid of the container.

Place the phone vertically in a container of silica-based cat litter.

8 **Wait 48 hours.**

Leave the phone in the drying agent for at least 48 hours. Do not attempt to turn it back on or charge it before then, or any residual water might cause a short circuit.

9 **Repeat.**

If the phone won't turn on after you try charging it, put it back in the drying agent for an additional 24 hours.

PRO TIPS

▶ One in five cell phone customers will at some point drop their phone in the toilet.

▶ Save silica gel packets from new shoe boxes and clothing purchases, emptying them into a container to use as an emergency cell phone drying chamber.

▶ Some studies show that leaving your cell phone to air-dry in front of a fan may be just as effective as using a drying agent.

HOW TO NAVIGATE WITHOUT GPS

IN THE WILDERNESS

Determining cardinal direction (the compass points) is the first critical step in wayfinding. Study the topography for the general direction of ancient glacial paths or predominant wind historically found in your location, and then use the multiple indicators that follow for better reliability.

- **Watch the sun.**
  The sun rises in the east and sets in the west—even in Australia. In the northern hemisphere, at midday the sun will be due south or a few degrees from due south, depending on time zone. In the southern hemisphere, it will be north/due north. At the equator, it will be overhead and north-south will be difficult to judge using this method.

- **Use the moon.**

  If a crescent moon is present, draw an imaginary vertical line connecting the two points of the crescent. Continue the line to the horizon. This point is due south (due north in the southern hemisphere).

- **Read the stars.**

  Draw an imaginary line between the two far-right stars of the Big Dipper, bottom to top. This line points to the North Star. Note, however, that due to wobbles in the Earth's rotation around its axis, the North Star is not due/true north.

- **Watch the weather.**

  Atmospheric circulation causes winds to blow in predictable directions, typically from west to east, though weather variability makes this method less reliable.

- **Listen for woodpeckers.**

  Woodpeckers peck the majority of their holes on the south sides of trees in the northern hemisphere. (They also peck on the other sides, though less frequently.) Check multiple trees before relying on this method.

- **Check tree stumps, flowers, and moss.**

  The rings on tree stumps will be wider on the south-facing side of stumps. Flowers will also generally face south, even on mostly cloudy days. Moss grows thicker and higher up on the north side of trees.

In a Snowstorm

- **Check the base of trees or poles.**
  The snow at the base of a tree or pole will display a crescent shape on the south side of the tree/pole, the result of melt from retained heat of the sun.

- **Check the edges of lakes.**
  Frozen, snow-covered lakes will display *sastrugi*—wind-driven ridges—from west to east.

How to Travel

Once compass points are known, begin walking.

- **Move north-south in valleys.**
  In many North American locations, mountain ranges and their valleys tend to run north-south, due to ancient glaciation and erosion from the retreat of ice toward the poles. (In Europe, they may run west to east.)

- **Move east-west along rivers.**
  Rivers tend to run east-west, though they may run north-south for long stretches.

- **Calculate time and distance.**
  A person walking through dense bush can cover 3–4 miles per day. In more forgiving terrain, covering 20 miles (or about 3 miles per hour) is possible.

- **Avoid climbing.**

  Elevation will add significant travel time. Hiking in mountain terrain will add an additional one-and-a-half minutes of travel time for each 30-foot rise in elevation.

IN A CITY

- **Check phone.**

  Even with no internet connection, your phone's compass app may be functional.

- **Observe flags.**

  Prevailing winds from the west will blow flags toward the east. Make sure the flags are on high buildings and not subject to swirling winds at street level.

- **Visit old churches.**

  Older Christian churches were constructed in a north-south orientation, with knaves running east-west. (This method is not effective for synagogues or mosques.)

- **Check satellite dishes.**

  In the northern hemisphere, satellite dishes face south, toward the equator, due to the orbit of communications satellites.

- **Examine old buildings.**

  Older buildings that have not been recently cleaned will have more soot on their west-facing sides. South facades may be more bleached from sun exposure.

- **Look at street signs.**

  While not always a reliable indicator of direction, numbered streets in U.S. cities tend to run north-south, while named streets run east-west. Eighty percent of cities have numbered streets running only one direction (either north or south, called the *Philadelphia system*) with New York City being the most well-known exception.

HOW TO SURVIVE
A DRONE ATTACK

MILITARY-STYLE DRONE

1 **Avoid initial detection.**

Drones can follow virtually any target once they know it is the right target. Your best hope for survival is to prevent the operator from identifying you in the first place.

2 **Stay off the phone.**

Military drones use a combination of visual and electronic surveillance to acquire and confirm targets. Do not make calls, send emails or texts, browse the Web, or use apps that can be connected to you personally. In most cases, the drone will not attack until the operator can confirm—either by sight or electronically—that the phone is actually being used by the intended target and not a family member or associate.

3 Choose cover carefully.

From 25,000 to 30,000 feet, a drone will circle a target endlessly; when one is low on fuel, it will be replaced by another. You will therefore be under constant surveillance. Enter a building only if it connects to a subway or other nearby buildings that provide multiple escape routes.

4 Change appearance.

Once indoors, change clothing and put on a hat before going out again.

5 Use weather.

Wait until conditions deteriorate before leaving a secure building. Military drones can operate in bad weather, but cloud cover, heavy rain, and snow and ice may prevent the operator from visually confirming a target.

6 Stay alert.

Drones are very difficult to detect visually, though anecdotal evidence suggests they can be heard under certain atmospheric conditions. If you suspect a strike is imminent, you will have just seconds to act.

7 Get underground.

The complete weapons systems of Predator and Raptor drones are classified, but they are equipped with high-explosive–tipped missiles. Your best chance of survival is in a hardened bunker below ground, in a deep cave, or in the basement of a stone or brick building.

DRONE SWARM

Multirotor-type drones are extremely maneuverable, and new technology, such as AI, allows them to *swarm*: fly collaboratively and follow targets autonomously. Take the following steps to avoid/survive an attack.

1 **Run quickly in a zigzag pattern.**

You cannot outrun a drone. However, very fast movement may confuse sensors on follow-type drones, allowing you to escape—unless some of the swarm is already out ahead of you.

Run in a zigzag pattern to confuse the drones' sensors.

2 **Move quickly into trees.**

Small drones are easily damaged and disabled by contact with obstructions. Run into a forest or other heavily wooded area where drones cannot fly easily. Note the drones may hover and be waiting when you break cover.

3 **Remain concealed.**

Small drones are limited by their small batteries, and most will lose power after about 30 minutes. If you can stay hidden, you may be able to outlast them.

4 **Use darkness.**

By FAA regulation, drones may not operate at night. Bad actors may ignore such rules, but drone cameras are not equipped to follow targets they cannot see. Sneak away after dark.

5 **Knock them out of the sky.**

Use a blanket, broom, or other object to swipe at drones when they get too close. Note, however, that multiple small drones may converge on a target all at once.

PRO TIPS

▶ Do not assume you are safe on a windy day. High-quality multirotor drones have effective stabilization mechanisms and can fly in high winds.

▶ Drones cannot operate in water (yet), so diving under the surface and swimming away may allow you to escape. The drones may hover and reacquire you upon resurfacing, however.

HOW TO SURVIVE A PRIVACY BREACH

HOW TO SURVIVE GETTING HACKED

1 Act immediately.

Most stolen data is sold on the Dark Web multiple times before it is used. The quicker you move to cancel accounts and change passwords, the less useful/valuable your information will be to each successive recipient.

2 Switch to your burner.

Keep a backup "burner" cell phone, paid for in cash and fully charged, on hand. Swap SIMs from your primary phone, if possible. Use this phone to contact credit card companies, banks, and other financial service companies to cancel accounts or change contact information. Or borrow a landline.

3 **Do not negotiate with hackers.**

Like spammers, most sophisticated hackers target thousands or tens of thousands of victims at once, hoping a tiny fraction will respond. If you are the target of a ransom demand, responding to thieves will only demonstrate that you are a weak, willing, or anxious victim, and draw their attention.

4 **Do not open emails or click on links.**

They may be forged and/or malicious.

5 **Assume your data is gone.**

Paying Bitcoin or other ransom is unlikely to get your data back. Hackers are not honorable and are unlikely to unlock your machine or restore your data, even if you pay. If you have made regular backups, buy a new machine and restore your data.

6 **Search the Web.**

An encryption key may have already been found and posted on the Web by a friendly source.

7 **Stay alert.**

Most identity thieves know their victims. Monitor family members and close friends for suspicious behavior such as newfound wealth, credit cards in your name, and knowledge of your most intimate moments.

PRO TIPS

- ▶ Two-factor authentication can be a useful security measure, but only if your phone remains in your possession or is itself not hacked.

- ▶ Activate both text and email alerts for all transactions from your financial institutions.

- ▶ Write passwords down on paper, but only in code. Consider a simple cypher: replace each letter of the alphabet with its numerical equivalent, and vice versa. Keep the paper list in a physical safe.

- ▶ Online sites that allow you to "lock" your credit are themselves targets for hackers.

- ▶ Using multiple credit cards, each with low credit limits, is more secure than one or two cards with high limits.

- ▶ One of the best ways you can avoid being hacked is simply to unplug your computer (and any other connected devices you might have in your home). Hackers cannot access a device that isn't powered up.

- ▶ A strategically placed piece of tape or cardboard over your computer's webcam won't prevent hacking, but it will prevent anyone from remotely viewing or recording the things that it sees.

HOW TO SURVIVE
IF YOU ARE DOXXED

Doxxing refers to the digital theft of personal information—
name, birthdate, address, social security number, usernames,
and passwords—to allow perpetrators to cyberbully, scam
and attack, and abuse you online. Doxxers generally use
personal information to gain access to and fake new social
media accounts, post false and embarrassing emails and
texts, and generally overwhelm victims with a barrage of
harmful and false posts and messages.

1 **Find a friend or professional IT person that you trust
to help you lock down your accounts–and avoid
looking at them if you are being actively doxxed.**
The problems doxxers cause can be emotionally taxing
and time consuming to fix—so appointing a third party
to help you control the situation may be better than
getting yourself more upset with direct involvement.

2 **Report the doxxing to the platform security team.**
All social media platforms, websites, and apps should be
able to help you quickly freeze your accounts, change
your passwords, remove damaging posts, and fix the
problem—and may even be able to track the doxxer down.

3 Report the crime to the police, FBI, or other authorities where appropriate.

Doxxing itself is not illegal; however if you are being threatened, intimidated, or harassed, you should report these crimes to the police (if local) or the FBI (if out of state).

4 Protect your privacy on social media platforms.

Keep your personal account private by only allowing friends and colleagues you know well to view your profile and posts.

5 Create individual logins for all of your online accounts.

Do not use major platforms (such as Facebook or Google) for logins on third-party apps, platforms, or websites. This will reduce your exposure.

6 Use a Virtual Private Network (VPN) when online to obscure your activity and data.

If you are not using a VPN, then your ISP and anyone or anything connected to your router has access to your data. A VPN encrypts your data so that it isn't visible to the outside world. There are multiple options, from free VPN services to those that will cost you around $10/month. Select a VPN that meets your needs (i.e., will allow you to connect multiple devices, etc.).

7 Install an anti-malware program on your computer and mobile devices.

This will prevent doxxers from using spyware to steal your personal info.

8   **Remove your personal info from all apps.**

Generally speaking, you do not have to use your actual name or identity in most apps. Leave the fields blank, or use an alias.

9   **Protect your email identity by using a "burner" email account.**

Use this email when registering for sites and apps that you don't need information from on a regular basis.

10   **Vary usernames and passwords.**

Ideally, you should use a different password for each of your online accounts. Do not use people's names or dates, and use synonyms and acronyms whenever possible. Use combinations of upper and lowercase letters, punctuation marks, numbers, and special characters liberally. Do not worry about forgetting your passwords—you can always reset them (in fact, changing your passwords regularly is highly recommended).

HOW TO SURVIVE A WIKILEAK

1   **Respond quickly.**

If the documents, videos, or images posted online are real (and can be proven to be so), apologize and say you have asked your family/friends/opponents for forgiveness. If the documents are false (or true but cannot be verified), vigorously deny them.

2 **Go on the attack.**

Accuse your enemies (personal, corporate, or international actors) of trying to embarrass you, ruin your life, or otherwise distract you from the important work you do.

3 **Circle your family around you.**

Gather your spouse, children, and any other available family members for a photo-op showing them standing around you looking proud and trusting. Invite the press to film you at a family picnic or sporting event. Present yourself as a solid family person whose family continues to support you.

4 **Do not lie.**

Providing inaccurate accounts of your activities could create a whole host of new issues.

5 **Quickly move on.**

When pressed about the scandal, say that you want to focus on "what's important—my family and my work."

6 **If the scandal persists, leave town, or take refuge in rehab.**

Escaping from view can be helpful—the news cycle and the internet's attention span are quick and will move on without you after a day or so. Alternatively, declare that you have a drug or alcohol dependency that drove you to act out, and then check into a secure and secluded rehab clinic. When you are back, appear in public and ask for forgiveness.

HOW TO SURVIVE IF YOUR SMART HOME OUTSMARTS YOU

Your connected home may begin to interfere with your life, first in small, seemingly innocuous ways and later in overt attempts to take over. Be prepared for the following danger signs.

1 **Your devices become more interesting than you are.**

Questions and conversation may be directed at your virtual voice assistant (Amazon Alexa, Google Assistant) and not at you. Facts and figures, weather forecasts, recipes, music, and philosophical musings about religion and the meaning of life can all be produced instantly by your Web-connected smart hub. If you feel ignored or left out at the table, your home may be replacing you.

2 **Your spouse becomes data-driven in the bedroom.**

Your partner may become obsessed with a sleep-tracking app and replace intimacy with metrics demanding 85 percent or better sleep efficiency. Bedtime may get progressively earlier. Bedroom conversation and "pillow talk" will adversely impact dynamic sleep scoring and may be eliminated. Late-night assignations will be recorded and will also have a negative sleep correlation.

3 **You become monitoring-fixated.**

The Smart Home can track everything, including on-the-fly energy usage. Your phone may bombard you with warnings and alerts about wasteful three-minute showers, frequent fridge openings, or excessively dark toast. You may become an energy scold, and relaxation will prove difficult.

4 **Your house has a "poltergeist."**

Lights change color without warning, the Instant Pot begins cooking, rock music switches to Muzak, and the front door unlocks itself. These and other automated actions follow "if this then that" (IFTTT) rules that you created but can no longer remember. This may cause you to become disoriented and confused.

5 **You outsource parenting.**

Your Smart Home may begin taking your place, sending automated instructions to kids, helping with their homework, and reading them audiobooks at bedtime. If they no longer ask where you are—or care—you may need to take evasive action.

IF YOUR HOME IS HACKED OR BECOMES SELF-AWARE AND TRIES TO TAKE OVER

1 **Turn off your cell phone.**

The Smart Home may use geolocation to monitor your position.

2 **Disable your virtual voice assistant.**

A hacker may use a WiFi-enabled toy to speak to your virtual assistant and command it to open the front door.

3 **Block security cameras.**

The Smart Home may use motion detection to track your movements. Cover lenses with clothing.

4 **Unplug your television.**

Your Smart TV may be listening to your conversations and sending data to a remote location.

5 **Light candles.**

The Smart Home may turn off all Smart bulbs, leaving you in total darkness.

6 **Disable your Smart Thermostat.**

The Smart Home may try to freeze or sweat you out. Remove the unit from the wall and disconnect all wires.

7 **Turn off the water supply.**

The Smart Home may attempt to control Smart Sinks and Smart Showers in an attempt to flood you out or cause damage.

8 **Remove the batteries from toys and baby monitors.**

Smart toys and monitors may surveil your activity and share it.

9 **Cancel your credit cards.**

The Smart Home may attempt to commit financial fraud, running up large bills by auto-ordering items using Amazon Dash and your Smart Fridge.

10 **Call for help.**

If you have voice over internet protocol (VOIP), it has probably been disabled. If a landline is available, call 911 and report your emergency. Alternatively, open a window and yell for help.

11 **Crawl out a window.**

If the Smart Home's security system has auto-locked doors, break the glass on a first-floor window and crawl to safety.

HOW TO SURVIVE AN OUT-OF-CONTROL AUTONOMOUS CAR

1 **Fasten your seat belt.**

As in a normal car, your best chance of survival in a wayward autonomous vehicle is to be buckled securely into the seat, front or rear.

2 **Sound the horn.**

If you are in the front seat, honk the horn repeatedly to alert other drivers to move out of your way. If no horn is present, or if you're in the back, see next step.

3 **Alert pedestrians.**

If the car has not prevented you from doing so, open the windows and yell a warning to pedestrians. If it has not been corrupted, the car's dataset should command it to avoid people and other obstacles.

4   **Remain calm.**

Unless the car had been hacked (see next step), its computer system should have a built-in fail-safe: when sensors are compromised and the system becomes confused, the car should slow down and pull over safely.

5   **Be alert for hacking.**

If the car's software has been hacked, it will act with confidence, not confusion. This situation is particularly dangerous, because the car's natural tendencies toward safety will be replaced with aggression. If the car speeds up, makes sharp turns, or tries to evade police, you may need to take additional action.

6   **Hit the kill switch.**

An autonomous vehicle should have a mechanical "kill" switch in a highly visible location: check the dash, center stack, or steering column (if one is present). This switch should either allow you to take control, or force the car to pull over safely. Later generations of autonomous cars may use a software kill switch, as a cost-cutting measure. This software may also be vulnerable to hacking.

7   **Jump.**

Leap out of the car only as a last resort, and only at low speed, and onto a soft surface such as a grass median (see **HOW TO JUMP FROM A MOVING CAR**). If the car is moving too fast, consider a car-to-car transfer (see **HOW TO JUMP FROM ONE CAR INTO ANOTHER**).

HOW TO SURVIVE A GRID COLLAPSE

In a true "black sky" event, 75 percent or more of the nation's high-voltage electrical transformers may be destroyed, either through a well-coordinated physical attack or via cyberwarfare. In this scenario, full recovery could take years. Even partial reconstruction of the grid may take many months or years, owing to long lead times in electrical equipment manufacturing, plus a lack of emergency stockpiles in the industry. Take the following steps.

1 **Remain calm.**

Unless you are in immediate physical danger from an active foreign invasion, stay put. You will need some time to learn the cause of the outage and extent of the damage. Do not rely on word of mouth for information, as it may be inaccurate rumor.

2 **Make contact.**

Use a battery-powered radio to monitor emergency broadcasts. Amateur (or ham) radio operators will be an invaluable source of information from across the country, and these radios can be easily powered by a generator. If you have one, use it.

3   **Gather emergency supplies.**

In addition to stockpiles of water and canned/dried foods, you will need:

- A generator and fuel, a solar array, or a small wind turbine

- A portable light source and sufficient batteries, both standard and rechargeable

- A camping stove and sufficient propane

- Matches

- Clothing for all seasons

- A full first aid kit

- A bicycle

- Maps

- Books and games

4   **Get reliable information.**

If power authorities and government officials are able to communicate with one another, the extent of the damage to the grid—and an estimate of the repair time—should be known relatively quickly, perhaps within weeks. This information will be broadcast, and should inform your decision to stay where you are or evacuate to a different location.

5 **Consult a map.**

Military bases have redundant power sources, plenty of supplies, and lots of security. These bases are likely to have "war-gamed" the situation and prepared accordingly. If you are unable or unwilling to stay put, and a base is nearby, consider making it your first destination.

6 **Travel during daylight hours, on foot or bicycle.**

Navigation at night will be extremely difficult and dangerous, and will waste batteries. Car travel should be avoided since gas will be unavailable and traffic lights inoperable.

7 **Move to an urban area.**

Power will be restored to denser cities and regions first, followed by less-dense locales, and then finally to more remote rural areas. Consider moving to a city near a major dam, such as (in the United States) Portland, Oregon, and Buffalo or Niagara Falls, New York.

HOW TO DEFEAT
A CYBERBULLY

1 **Do not respond.**

All bullies thrive on and feed on attention. Resist the urge to respond to intimidation. Unlike offline bullies, cyberbullies can gauge your reaction only by what you type/send.

2 **Find an ally.**

Reach out to a trusted confidant—even one whom you know only online—and explain your situation. If the authorities become involved, the ally will be able to confirm your side of the story.

3 **Keep good records.**

Make digital copies of all intimidating messages, photos, and videos. Print out text and emails to document bullying.

4 **Detach from accounts.**

Log out of all accounts and apps where the bully is pursuing you. Turn off all notifications. Set up filters in email to send all of the bully's messages to a specific folder, but do not delete them; they may be needed as evidence later.

5 **Keep devices minimally charged at all times.**

Low-power mode should limit background data fetches, and will deter needless app usage.

6 **Reduce data plan.**

Downgrade to the smallest data plan with the lowest speeds possible. Consider a "dumb" or flip phone to avoid unwanted or disturbing messages.

7 **Attempt a "cyber-break."**

Though seemingly impossible, begin to limit your time online. Start with five hours online a day, and slowly reduce time online by one hour a day for four days. Consider learning a new skill (cooking, painting, surgery) to fill your newly free time.

8 **Contact the police.**

If the bully hasn't given up, report his or her actions to authorities. Have evidence at hand.

HOW TO IDENTIFY FAKE NEWS

1 **Evaluate the URL.**

Sites that end in ".lo" or that append well-known news sites with ".com.co" tend to be biased and/or nothing but clickbait.

2 **Perform title and domain analysis.**

While not guaranteed indicators that the content is fake or biased, words like "wordpress" or "blogger" in the domain typically signify the site is a personal blog rather than an established news source. Many legitimate, freelance journalists do maintain their own blogs, so use your best judgment when evaluating the content.

3 **Check "About Us" section, or note its absence.**

Sites without clear ownership or contact information beyond a generic email address should be considered suspect.

4 **Beware of poor grammar, ALL CAPS, and excessive exclamation points!!!!**

Lack of copyediting and effective proofreading may indicate the source is biased or, in some cases, created by bots or automated aggregators.

5 **Check Snopes and Wikipedia.**

Enter the source name into these two sites, which may offer information on whether the content is legitimate or suspect/scammy. If you suspect a Wikipedia entry itself may be biased, click on "view history" in the top right corner to view its contributors.

6 **Monitor your emotions.**

Clickbait sites often used charged language (good and bad) to elicit an emotional response that will make you more likely to share the story or click on links. If you feel yourself becoming overly smug, self-satisfied, or angry, consider learning about the topic from another source.

7 **Resist clickbait if possible.**

Sites that have generally credible stories but use exaggerated, misleading, or "listy" headlines may be clickbait, profiting from each click-through or affiliate share made by a visitor. Some legitimate (or borderline legitimate) news sites may also use sensational headlines, so seek other sources to confirm the content of stories.

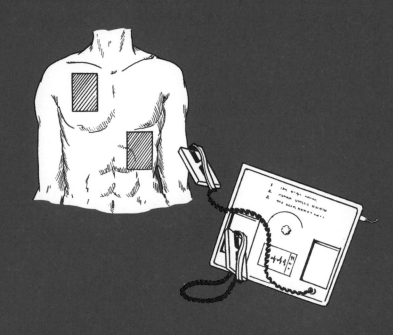

CHAPTER SIX

Critical Conditions

HOW TO USE A DEFIBRILLATOR TO RESTORE A HEARTBEAT

Defibrillation is the delivery of a powerful electrical shock to the heart. (The defibrillator is the device used in movies and TV shows: two handheld pads are placed on the victim's chest while an actor yells "Clear!") Once they were very heavy, expensive, and mostly found in hospitals; now smaller automatic external defibrillators (AEDs) can be found just about anywhere: at pools, gyms, airports, and other public places. Use of AEDs has become part of the American Heart Association's Basic Life Support (BLS) protocol that includes cardiopulmonary resuscitation (CPR). Chest compressions and mouth-to-mouth or mouth-to-valve resuscitation remain the most important components of BLS, and the rescuer should start CPR immediately after determining that a victim has become unconscious and has no pulse or respirations. A defibrillator should be used only for Sudden Cardiac Arrest (SCA), an electrical problem in the body that cannot be helped by CPR.

HOW TO USE A DEFIBRILLATOR

1 Turn on the defibrillator by pressing the appropriate button.

Most machines will provide both visual and voice prompts.

2 Remove the person's shirt and jewelry.

3 Apply the pads to the chest as shown in the diagram displayed on the machine's LED panel.

One pad should be placed on the upper right side of the chest, one on the lower left.

4 Plug the pads into the connector.

The defibrillator will analyze the patient's heart rhythm and determine if he/she needs a shock. Do not touch the patient at this time.

5 If the machine determines that a shock is needed, it will direct you—both audibly and with visual prompts—to deliver a shock, usually by pressing the appropriate button.

Before delivering a shock, make sure no one is touching the patient. The machine will automatically recheck the patient's heart rhythm again in two minutes to see whether or not the patient needs a second shock and, if so, will direct you to deliver another shock.

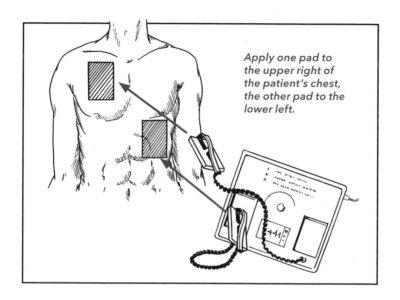

Apply one pad to the upper right of the patient's chest, the other pad to the lower left.

6 Check the patient's airway, breathing, and pulse between shocks.

If the patient still has no pulse and is not breathing, basic CPR should be performed by a qualified individual trained in BLS. If there is a pulse but the patient is not breathing, begin mouth-to-mouth resuscitation.

PRO TIP

In Sudden Cardiac Arrest, the heart's electrical signals become confused and the heart ceases to function. A person experiencing SCA will stop breathing; the pulse will slow, become "thready" (rapid and weak), or stop; and consciousness will be lost.

HOW TO PERFORM A TRACHEOTOMY

This procedure, technically called a *cricothyroidotomy*, should be undertaken only when a person with a throat obstruction is not able to breathe at all—no gasping sounds, no coughing—and only after you have attempted to perform the Heimlich maneuver (also called abdominal thrusts) three times without dislodging the obstruction and the victim becomes unconscious. Direct someone to call emergency services before starting the procedure.

WHAT YOU WILL NEED

▶ A first aid kit, if available; some kits may contain "trache" tubes.

▶ A razor blade, very sharp knife, or box cutter.

▶ A ballpoint pen with the inside (ink-filled tube) removed, or stiff paper or cardboard rolled into a tube.

You will not have time to sterilize your tools, so don't bother.

HOW TO PROCEED

1   Find the person's Adam's apple (thyroid cartilage).

2   Move your finger about one inch down the neck until you feel another bulge.

This is the cricoid cartilage. The indentation between the two is the cricothyroid membrane, where the incision will be made.

3   Make a three-quarter-inch horizontal incision.

Using the razor blade or knife, make the incision. The cut should be about half an inch deep. There should not be too much blood.

4   Open the incision.

Pinch the incision or place your finger inside to open it.

5   Insert the tube.

Place the tube in the incision, roughly one-half to one inch deep.

6   Breathe into the tube with two quick breaths.

Pause five seconds, and then give one breath every five seconds.

7   You will see the chest rise and the person may regain consciousness if you have performed the procedure correctly.

The person should be able to breathe on their own, albeit with some difficulty, until help arrives.

cricoid cartilage   **Adam's apple**

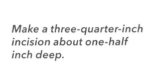

Find the indentation between the Adam's apple and the cricoid cartilage.

Make a three-quarter-inch incision about one-half inch deep.

Pinch the incision or insert your finger inside the slit to open it.

Insert your tube into the incision, roughly one-half to one inch deep.

HOW TO SAVE YOURSELF IF YOU ARE HAVING A HEART ATTACK

1   **Chew aspirin.**

As soon as you suspect a heart attack, thoroughly chew and swallow one aspirin tablet (325 mg), or four baby aspirins (81 mg). Chewing will allow the aspirin to enter the bloodstream more quickly. Heart attacks occur when the blood vessels supplying oxygen to the heart muscle become clogged. Aspirin will not stop the heart attack or remove the blockage, but it will prevent blood-clotting cells (platelets) from adding to the blockage.

2   **Alert others.**

If possible, tell people around you that you are having a heart attack. Instruct them to call emergency services.

3   **Decrease the heart's oxygen consumption.**

Stop all activity. The faster your heart pumps, the more oxygen it uses up. Think calming thoughts about bringing your heart rate down to one beat per second. If you have a watch with a second hand, focus on the second hand. For each second, think or say quietly "heartbeat." Repeat.

4 **Increase oxygen delivery to the heart.**

Lie down on the ground. Elevate your legs to keep as much blood pooled around your heart as possible; this will decrease the work your heart must do to pump blood. Open the windows to increase the room's oxygen level. If you have access to an oxygen tank, place the nasal cannula under your nose, turn the knob to four liters (or until you feel air coming through the nasal prongs), and take deep, slow breaths through your nose and out your mouth.

5 **Perform cough-CPR.**

Breathe, and then cough every three seconds. Take a breath in through your nose, think "heartbeat, heartbeat, heartbeat," and then cough. Repeat. Coughing will deter fainting and help you stay conscious until conventional CPR can be administered.

PRO TIP

Do not consume food or water. You may need a hospital procedure to "unclog" your arteries, and food or liquids in your system complicate treatment.

HOW TO DELIVER A BABY IN THE BACK OF A CAR

Before you attempt to deliver a baby, use your best efforts to get to a hospital. There really is no way to know exactly when the baby is ready to deliver, so even if you think you may not have enough time to get to the hospital, you probably do. Even the "water breaking" is not a sure sign that birth will happen immediately. The water is actually amniotic fluid within the amniotic sac that the baby floats in; birth can occur many hours after the water breaks. Babies basically deliver themselves, and they will come out of the womb when they are ready. However, if you leave too late or get stuck in traffic and you must deliver the baby on your own, here are the basic concepts.

1 **Prep back seat.**

Have clean dry towels, a clean shirt, or something similar on hand to place under the mother.

2 **Guide the head.**

As the baby moves out of the womb, its head, the largest part of its body, will open the cervix so the rest of the baby can pass through. As the baby moves through the birth canal and out of the mother, guide it out by supporting the head and then the body. Try to control the head so it emerges slowly to avoid tearing the mother.

3   **Clear airway.**

Do not slap the baby's behind to make it cry; the baby will breathe on its own. If necessary, clear any fluid out of the baby's mouth with your fingers or gently squeeze the baby's cheeks.

4   **Keep baby warm and dry.**

When the baby is out of the mother, dry it off and keep it warm; next to the mother's skin is the ideal spot. The umbilical cord will still be attached at this point.

5   **Tie umbilical cord.**

Wait 30 seconds after birth before tying the cord, to allow blood to pass from the placenta to the baby. To tie off the umbilical cord, use a piece of string (a shoelace works well). Tie off the cord several inches from the baby. It is not necessary to cut the umbilical cord, unless you are hours away from the hospital. In that event, you can safely cut the cord by tying it in another place a few inches closer to the mother and cutting between the knots. Leave the cord alone until you get to the hospital.

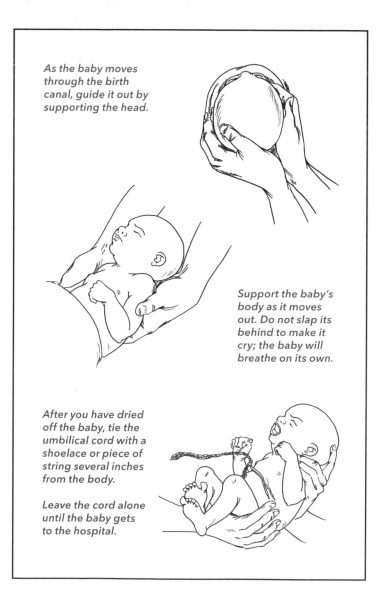

As the baby moves through the birth canal, guide it out by supporting the head.

Support the baby's body as it moves out. Do not slap its behind to make it cry; the baby will breathe on its own.

After you have dried off the baby, tie the umbilical cord with a shoelace or piece of string several inches from the body.

Leave the cord alone until the baby gets to the hospital.

6   **Watch for placenta.**

The placenta will usually follow the baby in as few as 3 minutes or as many as 30 minutes. If the placenta delivers, massage the uterus firmly to decrease the amount of maternal bleeding. If the placenta does not deliver spontaneously or by gentle traction on the cord, wait until you get to the hospital to have it delivered. Remember to keep the baby warm while you are focused on the mother.

PRO TIP

If the baby's feet or buttocks are coming first, this is a breech delivery. Since the head is the largest part of the baby, the danger is that it may get stuck after the body delivers. Today, most breech babies are delivered by cesarean section. Generally, by a doctor exam or an ultrasound, the mother will know in advance if there will be a breech or other abnormal presentation. In this situation, the safest option (for both mother and baby) is to get to the hospital rather than attempt delivery yourself. Breech births are uncommon, occurring in only about 3 percent of deliveries.

HOW TO SURVIVE AN EARTHQUAKE

1 **If you are indoors, stay there.**

- ▶ Get under a heavy desk or table and hang on to it; the next best place is in a hallway or against an inside wall.

- ▶ If you cannot get to a safer location, crouch down and cover your head and neck with your arms.

- ▶ Stay clear of windows, fireplaces, and heavy furniture or appliances.

- ▶ Get out of the kitchen, which is a dangerous place.

- ▶ Do not run downstairs or rush outside while the building is shaking, or while there is danger of falling and hurting yourself or being hit by falling glass or debris.

2 **If you are outside, get into the open.**

- ▶ Move to the center of the street.

- ▶ Get away from buildings, power lines, chimneys, and anything else that might fall on you.

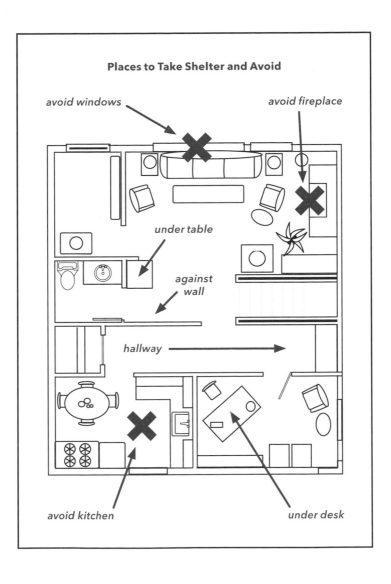

Places to Take Shelter and Avoid

avoid windows

avoid fireplace

under table

against wall

hallway

avoid kitchen

under desk

3   **If you are driving, stop, but carefully.**

- ▶ Move your car as far out of traffic as possible.

- ▶ Do not stop on or under a bridge or overpass, or under trees, light posts, power lines, or signs.

- ▶ Stay inside your car until the shaking stops. When you resume driving, watch for breaks in the pavement, fallen rocks, and bumps in the road at bridge approaches. Avoid bridges and overpasses.

4   **If you are in a mountainous area, watch out for falling debris.**

Beware of falling rocks, landslides, trees, and other debris that could be loosened by quakes.

5   **After the quake stops, check for injuries and apply the necessary first aid or seek help.**

Do not attempt to move seriously injured persons unless they are in further danger of injury. Cover them with blankets and seek medical help for serious injuries.

6   **Put on a pair of sturdy thick-soled shoes.**

If available, don protective footwear to help navigate broken glass and other sharp materials.

7   **Check for hazards.**

- ▶ Put out fires in your home or neighborhood immediately.

- ▶ Gas leaks: shut off the main gas valve only if you suspect a leak because of broken pipes or odor. Do not use matches, lighters, camp stoves or barbecues, electrical equipment, or appliances until you are sure there are no gas leaks. They may create a spark that could ignite leaking gas and cause an explosion and fire. Do not turn on the gas again if you turned it off—let the gas company do it.

- ▸ Damaged electrical wiring: shut off power at the control box if there is any danger to house wiring.

- ▸ Downed or damaged utility lines: do not touch downed power lines or any objects in contact with them.

- ▸ Spills: clean up any spilled medicines, drugs, or other harmful materials such as bleach, lye, or gas.

- ▸ Downed or damaged chimneys: approach with caution and do not use a damaged chimney (it could start a fire or let poisonous gases into your house).

- ▸ Fallen items: beware of items tumbling off shelves when you open closet and cupboard doors.

8 **Check food and water supplies.**

Do not eat or drink anything from open containers near shattered glass. If the power is off, plan meals to use up frozen foods or foods that will spoil quickly. Food in the freezer should be good for at least a couple of days. If the water is off you can drink from water heaters, toilet tanks (but not toilet bowls), melted ice cubes, or canned vegetables. Avoid drinking water from swimming pools and spas.

9 **Be prepared for aftershocks.**

Another quake, larger or smaller, may follow.

PRO TIPS

▸ Use your cell phone only for a medical or fire emergency—you could tie up the cell network needed for emergency response. If the network is down or congested, send someone for help.

▸ Do not expect firefighters, police, or paramedics to help you immediately. They may not be available.

▸ If you are trapped in a building, signal rescuers by tapping repeatedly on a pipe or other metal object.

HOW TO SURVIVE A TORNADO

ON FOOT IN THE OPEN

1 **Get to a structure.**

Find shelter in the nearest building—a home, office, school, or other engineered structure—and take cover (see below).

2 **If you cannot reach a structure, lie down and cover your head.**

If you are outdoors when the tornado strikes and cannot get inside, lie down flat in a ditch or low-lying area and put your hands over your head.

IN A VEHICLE

1 **Stay in the car.**

You will have absolutely no protection on foot, and likely will be unable to stand anyway.

If you cannot reach a structure, lie down in a ditch and cover your head.

2   **Drive to a structure only if there is no traffic.**

If you are on a rural road with decent visibility, quickly drive to an engineered structure (preferably one with a basement) and take cover.

3   **Drive out of the tornado's path.**

If you are in a car in the middle of nowhere, can see the tornado clearly, and no structures are nearby, asscss its motion. If it is moving toward you (it is not moving left or right with respect to your line of sight, but merely getting larger and staying at the same azimuth angle), drive quickly away from the tornado's path in a southerly direction. Driving to the north of the path will likely put you in very heavy rain and large hail.

4   Get in the back seat.

If you are stuck in traffic in the path of a tornado, or are in blinding rain with no visibility, move to the back seat of the car, away from the windshield. Crawl onto the floor and curl into a fetal position. Do not leave the car, attempt to get under an overpass, or lie down in a ditch: you may be hit by flying debris, including your own vehicle.

IN A HOME WITH A FOUNDATION AND BASEMENT

1   Move to the basement or an underground storm shelter, if available.

Close the door behind you.

2   Stay away from windows, if any are present.

3   Keep shoes on.

You will need them to protect your feet from broken glass, nails, wood shards, and other debris.

4   Put on a sports helmet, if you have one.

5   Get under a mattress or table.

Take shelter to protect yourself from falling debris.

PRO TIP

PRO TIP

Do not open windows to "equalize the pressure." Homes are not airtight, and opening windows will simply allow more wind to enter the house and potentially blow down walls.

IN A HOME WITH NO BASEMENT

- **Move to an interior room.**

  Move toward the interior of the building. Keep as many walls as possible between you and the tornado to protect you from projectiles. Bathrooms are good choices: pipes in walls may offer some extra protection and stability.

IN A SCHOOL, OFFICE BUILDING, OR ENGINEERED STRUCTURE WITH NO BASEMENT

- **Move to an interior room on the lowest floor, and stay away from windows.**

  Avoid auditoriums and gymnasiums: roofs on such rooms have historically been among the first to fail during tornados.

IN A STRUCTURE NOT DESIGNED TO SURVIVE HIGH WINDS

- **Evacuate immediately on foot.**
  If you are in a vulnerable structure such as a barn or mobile home, and determine that you are in the path of the tornado, find a neighbor with a sturdier structure and take shelter. Ideally this structure should be within walking or running distance.

PRO TIPS

- ► Carefully consider whether you can make it to a protective structure by car before choosing to drive. It is usually impossible to know very far in advance if you are directly in the tornado's path; warning areas are typically 200 square miles, and massive traffic jams caused by evacuees have been hit by tornadoes, resulting in fatalities.

- ► Most tornadoes last only a few minutes and travel at about 30 mph, covering just a few miles.

- ► While a tornado warning may occur just minutes before the storm arrives at a location, hurricanes may be forecast further in advance, providing more time for evacuation. If a hurricane evacuation order is given for your location, your safest course of action is to follow the order and leave the area.

HOW TO DEAL WITH A DOWNED POWER LINE

High-voltage power lines can come crashing down during severe storms.

IN A CAR

If you are in a car that has come into contact with a downed line or pole, call for help and remain inside the vehicle until assistance arrives.

1 **If you must get out, open the door.**

If there is a fire or severe injury and you cannot wait for help, open the car door. Do not allow any part of your body to come into contact with the ground while you are touching any part of the car.

2 **Jump.**

Climb up onto the seat. Keep your arms by your sides and leap out and away from the car, landing with both feet on the ground; follow directions below.

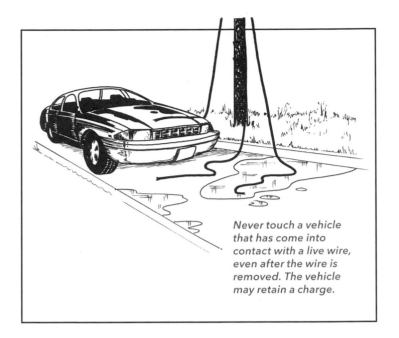

Never touch a vehicle that has come into contact with a live wire, even after the wire is removed. The vehicle may retain a charge.

ON FOOT

1 **Do not touch anything.**

Assume that all power lines are live. Stay far away from downed lines (and anything in contact with them), even if they are not sparking, humming, or "dancing."

2 **Move away slowly.**

Electricity travels through the ground in all directions from the point where a live wire touches the ground. Voltage decreases as distance from the wire touching the ground increases. Shuffle with your feet close together and keep the soles of your shoes on the ground.

3 Do not run.

Running or taking large steps may result in the conducting of electricity from one leg at one voltage to another leg at another voltage, increasing the potential for severe injury or death.

PRO TIPS

▸ Current can travel through any conductive material, including water, metal, wood, aluminum, string, and plastics.

▸ Water on the ground is especially dangerous as it can provide a "channel" from the power line to you.

▸ An electrical shock can also occur when a person comes in contact with the charged particles near a high-voltage line; direct contact is not necessary for electrocution to occur.

▸ Never touch a vehicle that has come in contact with a live wire—it may still retain a charge.

▸ Never assume that a non-sparking wire is safe. Power may be restored by automated equipment without warning, causing a "dead" wire to become dangerous. Stay away from downed lines even if you know they are not electric lines—the line could have come in contact with an electric line when it fell, causing the downed line to be "hot."

▸ If a person comes into contact with a live wire, do not touch them: you may be shocked also. Call for help.

HOW TO SURVIVE A WILDFIRE

Often the safest place in a wildfire is an area that has already burned—what firefighters call "the black." If you are in the black, carefully consider any decision to leave it.

1 **Determine wind direction.**

Observe smoke from the fire carefully to see which way it is being blown. Look as high in the sky as possible, where smoke direction is less affected by contours in the terrain or pockets of intense heat on the ground. Watch for strong rotation in the smoke plume above the fire. If you observe rotation, this indicates potential formation of a large fire whirl, which may move independently of the main fire.

2 **Determine slope.**

If you have the option, travel downslope. Hot air masses created by intense wildfires rise, and fires tend to spread more quickly uphill and burn hotter, making higher elevations more prone to ignition and more dangerous. Valley areas are more likely to hold moisture and contain less-combustible vegetation.

3 **Search for a firebreak.**

As you travel, look for a firebreak: paved or gravel road, clear-cut area created by the Forest Service, boulder field, or body of water. These areas may provide temporary safety from heat and flames until help arrives. Large rock outcroppings can also shield you from the heat emitted by the fire.

4 **Locate green trees.**

Large trees retain more moisture than grass or dry scrub, and may be a good alternative if no firebreak can be reached. In regions of severe drought, however, dry trees may be highly combustible.

5 **Move quickly.**

Wind-driven wildfires or fires burning up hills can move many times faster than a person can run, so use a vehicle if one is available. If on foot and you fear you are being overtaken, cover exposed skin with dry clothing and seek a safe path through the leading edge of the fire into an area that has already burned.

6 **Dig a fire trench.**

If you are surrounded and have no means of escape, move to an area of depression in the surrounding ground. Dig a hole in the side of the slope, place a tarp or blanket over the hole, cover it with dirt, and then crawl under the tarp into the hole. Alternatively, dig a trench two to three feet deep, lay down in it with your feet facing the direction of the flames, and cover yourself with dirt. Leave an air hole, and wait for the fire to travel over you. Avoid gullies that are oriented down the hill: these tend to channel hot air and fire upwards.

PRO TIPS

- ▶ Do not cover your mouth with a wet cloth: the superheated air from a forest fire may make breathing difficult or impossible, but dry air is less dangerous to the lungs than wet air.

- ▶ The coolest air is nearest to the ground. If you are caught and have only seconds to act, lie face down on the ground with your feet facing the oncoming fire. Dig a small depression for your face so you can breathe, and cover your back with any coats or extra clothing.

HOW TO SURVIVE A FLASH FLOOD OR LEVEE BREAK

1 **Move to higher ground immediately.**

Low-lying areas such as valleys, spillways, and areas around creeks, streams, and rivers flood first.

2 **Listen.**

Water moving quickly in a confined space may sound like a roaring jet engine or a freight train. If you hear a loud, sustained noise, flooding is imminent.

3 **Avoid saturated ground.**

Sodden terrain cannot absorb additional water. If you are standing on damp or wet ground, move to a drier area quickly. Note, however, that hard-packed sand or mud may also have limited ability to absorb excess water. Dry washes in the desert are especially dangerous and should be avoided if you hear thunder, even if the weather in your location is clear.

4 **Find shelter.**

Avoid being caught in the open. Locate a sturdy building, preferably one made of reinforced concrete and three stories or higher. Get as high as possible—including on the roof. Avoid any attic without roof access. Avoid mobile homes or structures without foundations, and cars, which may be swept away in just six inches of fast-moving water.

5 **Watch for debris.**

Floodwaters—even shallow water—may carry submerged debris that can knock you off your feet, and may contain dangerous chemicals. If you must cross running water, link arms in a human chain, or use a guide rope.

6 **Signal for rescue.**

Use a cell phone to call for help, or wave a cloth or piece of clothing to rescuers.

HOW TO SURVIVE A TSUNAMI

A tsunami (from the Japanese word meaning "harbor wave") is a series of traveling ocean waves of extremely long length generated by geological disturbances (earthquakes, underwater volcanic eruptions, landslides) and atmospheric conditions that cause sudden changes in barometric pressure (meteotsunamis). They can form hundreds or even thousands of miles away. The waves have been known to range from 50 to 100 feet in height.

1 If you are near the ocean, be aware of the warning signs of an approaching tsunami:

RISE OR FALL IN SEA LEVEL Often, coastal waters may be drawn back a considerable distance, leaving the seafloor bare. Rapidly receding water is a sign that a tsunami is imminent, though its wave height may be impossible to predict.

SHAKING GROUND Earthquakes do not always cause tsunamis, but in coastal zones they should be expected. A buoy-based tsunami warning system may not always be present or functioning properly, so prepare to evacuate. It may take several minutes to many hours after an earthquake for a tsunami to strike land.

LOUD, SUSTAINED ROAR Large waves moving from the deep ocean into shallow waters may be accompanied by a loud, "freight-train" type sound. However, towering waves may not appear especially high from a distance, and their height may increase rapidly based on topographic characteristics of the shoreline. Bays with narrow inlets are especially vulnerable. If you can see a wave approaching, assume you cannot outrun it.

2 **If you are on a boat in a small harbor and you have sufficient warning of an approaching tsunami, move it quickly.**

Your first choice should be to dock and reach high ground. Your second choice is to take your boat far into open water, away from shore where it might be thrown into the dock or the land. Tsunamis cause damage when they move from deeper to more shallow waters; the waves back up against one another at the shallow shelf. Often tsunamis are not even felt in deep water, and you may be unaware of one.

3   **If you are on land, seek higher ground immediately.**

Move to higher ground immediately and keep going, with an absolute minimum safe elevation of 30 feet above sea level as your guide. Tsunamis can move faster than a person can run. Get away from the coastline as quickly as possible. Avoid areas near bays, creeks, and rivers, as these waters may rise rapidly.

4   **If you are in a high-rise hotel or apartment building on the coastline and cannot get to higher ground away from the shore, move to a high floor of the building.**

The upper floors of a high-rise building can provide safe refuge. The third floor (or higher) of a reinforced concrete structure may be a safer choice than trying to navigate a clogged evacuation route. Select a building that has its longest side perpendicular, not parallel, to the shore.

5   **If you have no better options, get in a car, buckle the seat belt, and keep the windows closed.**

The car will be swept up in the wave, but its steel frame should provide some limited, temporary protection from debris in the floodwaters. The car is likely to be carried some distance, and may float until the windows are penetrated.

PRO TIPS

▶ The first tsunami wave may not be the largest in the series of waves.

▶ Tsunamis can travel up rivers and streams that lead to the ocean.

▶ Flooding from a tsunami can extend inland 1,000 feet or more, covering large expanses of land with water and debris.

▶ Tsunamis are often mistakenly referred to as tidal waves, but they are not the same thing. Tsunamis are not related to the gravitational forces that cause tides and, therefore, tidal waves.

HOW TO SURVIVE A VIRAL OUTBREAK OR SUPER-FLU

IF YOU ARE NOT INFECTED

1   **Get the flu vaccine, if available.**

Even if not 100 percent effective, it may lessen the duration and severity of infection.

2   **Avoid human contact.**

Infected people may transmit the virus before they display symptoms.

3   **Stay inside.**

Remaining indoors will limit your exposure to people and objects, both potential flu vectors.

4   **Do not touch anything.**

Most viruses are transmitted through hand contact, not through the air. The average adult may touch 30 objects every 60 seconds, and a child may touch her nose or mouth every 3 minutes. Flu virus may remain infectious for several hours "in the wild."

5 **Wear gloves.**

If you must leave home, wear gloves. If disposable, throw them away when you reach a non-infectious area. If not, launder in hot water.

6 **Wear a surgical face mask.**

Face masks may reduce the chance of infection via airborne flu droplets, especially in enclosed settings such as homes or hospitals. Airborne infection, however, is not the most common flu vector (see step 4 on this list).

7 **Wear a respirator.**

If worn correctly, an N95 respirator mask (sold in hardware stores) may be more effective in preventing flu transmission than a surgical mask—and hotter and more uncomfortable. The mask must fit snugly against the skin. All masks, regardless of type, are single use and should be thrown away after wearing once. Masks will also prevent you from touching your mouth and nose.

8 **Wash hands regularly.**

Handwashing with warm water and soap for 15–20 seconds is the most effective means of preventing transmission. If handwashing is impossible, disinfect hands with alcohol wipes.

Limit exposure.

Avoid places where children gather.

Avoid recirculated air.

Cough into your elbow.

Use only your own towel.

Disinfect everyday objects.

doorknobs

light switches

faucets

IF YOU ARE INFECTED

1 **Stay inside.**

Do not leave home until you have been fever-free for at least 24 hours without the use of fever-reducing medicine.

2 **Monitor symptoms.**

Flu symptoms include fever, cough, sore throat, congestion or runny nose, body aches, headache, chills, and fatigue. You may also have vomiting and diarrhea.

3 **Stay hydrated.**

Drink plenty of fluids—64 ounces of water or broth per day is recommended for adults. Consuming excessive fluids may result in hyponatremia, or a deficiency of sodium in the blood.

4 **Take an antiviral medication.**

Your doctor may prescribe an antiviral medication, which may lessen the severity of the illness. These medications are most effective if taken early in the flu cycle.

5 **Know when to go to the hospital.**

A super-flu may cause complications that can require hospitalization. These include difficulty breathing or shortness of breath, pain or pressure in the chest or abdomen, dizziness and confusion, or severe or persistent vomiting.

HOW TO SURVIVE NUCLEAR FALLOUT

1   **Assess bomb type.**

Significant fallout is a danger from ground-detonated nuclear weapons, not those detonated aboveground (airburst munitions). If you are outside the radius of initial destruction from an airburst bomb, you may not be in imminent danger.

2   **Remain calm.**

The danger of radioactive fallout from a ground-based nuclear detonation decreases with distance from ground zero. Except with a particularly high-yield weapon, unless you are within a mile of the blast, you are unlikely to be in imminent danger from the blast. However, the fallout plume can be dangerous to a distance of several miles downwind for those outside.

3   **Monitor wind direction.**

Fallout is dispersed by prevailing winds. If you are within 10 miles and downwind of the blast site, consider moving laterally—quickly—but only if it is safe to do so. To determine prevailing wind direction, tear a tissue into small strips and toss above you, noting which direction the strips are carried.

4 **Find shelter.**

If you are inside, stay there. If you are outside, quickly survey surrounding buildings. Locate the largest, sturdiest nearby structure, preferably one made of stone, brick, or concrete. Keep doors and windows closed. Avoid wood-framed buildings.

5 **Move to the basement.**

If no basement is available, move to the center of the structure, as far as possible from the building's sides and roof.

6 **Monitor a dosimeter.**

Radiation has no smell or taste, and it is undetectable without specialized equipment. If a dosimeter is available, monitor it carefully. One hundred rads per hour may result in fatal radiation poisoning in less than a day.

7 **Conserve water and food.**

Take small sips, and eat sparingly. If necessary, you are likely to be evacuated within a day or two, so stockpiling supplies is probably unnecessary. Water in the toilet tank can be used for drinking if needed. Do not drink from the bowl.

8   **Listen to the radio for emergency instructions.**
The nature of the attack and the government response should become clear within several hours. You will be told when it's safe to go outside and, if evacuation is necessary, you'll be told the best path to follow.

PRO TIP

Radiation attenuates over time. Many radioactive particles decay following the rule of sevens: After 7 hours, radioactivity will be reduced by a factor of 10 compared to 1 hour; in 2 days, the levels will have dropped by a factor of 100. After 2 weeks, it will be reduced by a factor of 1,000.

HOW TO SURVIVE HEAT EXHAUSTION

Heat exhaustion indicators include profuse sweating, fatigue, dizziness, general confusion, and muscle cramps. Other signs may include very dark urine (yellow or brown) and increased heart rate. Take the following steps.

1 **Stop all activity.**

Sit down in a shady or cool spot and rest. Sitting will also reduce the chances of injury, should you pass out.

2 **Remove tight-fitting clothing.**

This will increase circulation and promote cooling.

3 **Cool your body.**

The fastest way to bring the body's temperature down is full immersion in cool water. Any water below body temperature is effective, though colder is better. If immersion is impossible, soak clothing that is in contact with skin, or use wet rags.

4   **Begin fanning.**

Fan yourself, or instruct others to fan you, using items such as magazines, books, paper maps, hats, and clothing. Fanning speeds up skin cooling by increasing the rate of evaporation.

5   **Rehydrate slowly.**

Take small sips of water—don't gulp. Replace depleted minerals with a banana or sports drinks, if available.

6   **Track urination.**

Urination indicates the kidneys have regained normal function. Continue treatment, and when possible, move to an air-conditioned environment.

HOW TO TREAT FROSTBITE

Frostbite is a condition caused by the freezing of water molecules in skin cells, which occurs in very cold temperatures. It is characterized by white, waxy skin that feels numb and hard. More severe cases result in a bluish-black skin color, and the most severe cases result in gangrene, which will likely lead to amputation. Affected areas are generally fingertips and toes, as well as the nose, ears, and cheeks. Frostbite should be treated by a doctor. In an emergency, take the following steps before reaching professional medical care.

1 **Remove wet clothing.**

Dress the area with warm, dry clothing.

2 **Immerse frozen areas in warm water.**

Soak in 100–105° Fahrenheit water or apply warm compresses.

3 **If warm water is not available, wrap gently in warm blankets.**

4 **Avoid direct heat.**

Direct heat from sources including electric or gas fires, heating pads, and hot water bottles may cause burns and tissue damage.

5 **Never thaw the affected area if there is any risk of refreezing.**

This can cause more severe tissue damage.

6 **Do not rub frostbitten skin.**

7 **Take a pain reliever such as aspirin or ibuprofen during rewarming to lessen the pain.**

Rewarming will be accompanied by a severe burning sensation. There may be skin blistering and soft tissue swelling, and the skin may turn red, blue, or purple in color. When skin is pink and no longer numb, the area is thawed.

8 **Apply sterile dressings to the affected areas.**

Place the dressing between fingers or toes if they have been affected. Try not to disturb any blisters, wrap rewarmed areas to prevent refreezing, and have the patient keep thawed areas as still as possible.

9 **Get medical treatment as soon as possible.**

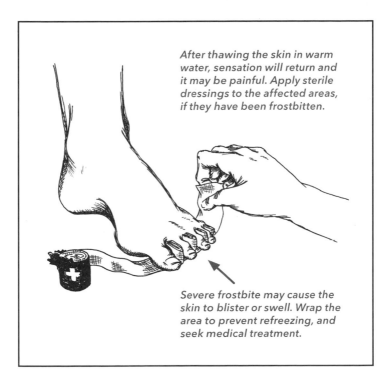

After thawing the skin in warm water, sensation will return and it may be painful. Apply sterile dressings to the affected areas, if they have been frostbitten.

Severe frostbite may cause the skin to blister or swell. Wrap the area to prevent refreezing, and seek medical treatment.

HOW TO TREAT FROSTNIP

Frostnip is the early warning sign of frostbite. Frostnip is characterized by numbness and a pale coloring of the affected areas. It can be safely treated by gentle external warming.

1   **Remove wet clothing.**

2 Immerse the affected areas.

Soak the areas in warm water (100–105° Fahrenheit) or air.

3 Do not allow the patient to control warm air or water temperature.

Numb areas are unlikely to feel heat and can be burned.

4 Continue treatment until skin is pink and sensation returns.

HOW TO AVOID FROSTBITE AND FROSTNIP

▶ Keep the body, and especially extremities, covered with layered clothing in cold weather. Avoid cotton, which draws body heat away from skin when wet or damp from perspiration.

▶ Protect all exposed skin and keep yourself hydrated.

▶ Mittens will keep your hands warmer than gloves.

▶ Blood circulation equals heat circulation: avoid tight footwear.

HOW TO TREAT A LEG FRACTURE

Most leg injuries are only sprains, but the treatment for both sprains and fractures is the same.

1 If skin is broken, do not touch or put anything on the wound.

You must avoid infection. If the wound is bleeding severely, try to stop the flow of blood by applying steady pressure to the affected area with sterile bandages or clean clothing.

2 Do not move the injured leg.

You need to splint the wound to stabilize the injured area.

3 Find two stiff objects of the same length.

Use wood, plastic, or folded cardboard for the splints.

4 Position the splints so that they span above and below the injured area.

Place under the leg, or on the side if moving the leg is too painful. The joint above and below the injury should be immobilized if possible.

5   **Tie the splints.**

Use string, rope, belts, or torn clothing—whatever is available.

6   **Do not tie the splints too tightly.**

This may cut off circulation. You should be able to slip a finger under the rope or fabric. If the splinted area becomes pale or white, loosen the ties.

7   **Have the injured person lie flat on their back.**

This helps blood continue to circulate and may prevent shock.

SYMPTOMS OF A FRACTURE, SPRAIN, OR DISLOCATION

- ▸ Difficult or limited movement
- ▸ Swelling
- ▸ Bruising of the affected area
- ▸ Severe pain
- ▸ Numbness
- ▸ Severe bleeding
- ▸ A visible break of bone through the skin

Do not move the injured leg.

Find two objects of the same length— wood, plastic, or folded cardboard.

Place the splints above and below the injured area.

Tie the splints with string, rope, or belts, whatever is available.

Do not tie the splints too tightly. You should be able to slip one finger under the binding material.

WHAT TO AVOID

▶ Do not push at, probe, or attempt to clean an open fracture; this can cause infection.

▶ Do not move the injured person unless absolutely necessary. Treat the fracture and then go get help.

▶ If the person must be moved, be sure the injury is completely immobilized first.

PRO TIP

Do not attempt to move or reset a broken bone; this will cause severe pain and may complicate the injury. However, if you are unable to stop bleeding from an open fracture with pressure only, straightening the limb into its natural shape may be lifesaving.

HOW TO TREAT A BULLET OR KNIFE WOUND

Bullets, knives, and other penetrating objects are common causes of life-threatening hemorrhage and other injuries. Although acting quickly to control external bleeding can be lifesaving, some sources of bleeding cannot be controlled in the field. Prompt transport to a hospital for definitive care is recommended.

1 **Do not remove knives or other impaled objects.** The object may be lodged against a blood vessel and removal may increase bleeding.

2 **Control external bleeding by using a combination of techniques.**

DIRECT PRESSURE

Most bleeding from extremity or scalp wounds can be controlled using direct pressure.

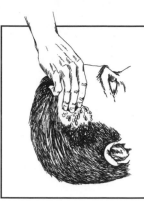

Apply pressure directly to bleeding surfaces. Using fingertips rather than palms is more effective for scalp wounds. Press on bleeding arterioles (small squirting vessels).

- Apply pressure to the wound with clean gauze or cloth, and hold it for at least several minutes.

- Wear sterile gloves if available.

- Do not use direct pressure on the eye.

- Direct pressure will not stop bleeding in the chest or abdomen; see the **IF THE WOUND IS TO THE CHEST** section that follows for instructions.

- If an impaled object remains in the wound, apply pressure on either side of the wound without removing the object.

LIMB ELEVATION

- If the wound is in an extremity, elevate it above the heart to decrease pressure at the site and help reduce bleeding.

- If the victim is in shock from blood loss—exhibiting a decreased level of consciousness, rapid weak pulse, pale or clammy skin, fast shallow breathing—the victim should remain flat while the extremity is elevated.

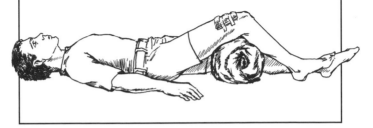

If the injury is in a limb, use pressure to control the bleeding, and elevate the limb. Dress the wound to prevent the spread of infection.

PRESSURE POINTS

If direct pressure and elevation are not controlling bleeding, apply pressure to the artery that supplies blood to the injured area, as follows:

▶ The brachial artery supplies blood to the upper extremities. Compress the artery using firm pressure with two or three fingers on the pulse point just below the armpit on the inside of the upper arm.

▶ The femoral artery supplies blood to the lower extremities. Compress the artery in the groin: feel for the pulse between the hip bone and the pubic area. Direct pressure to the bleeding site can be applied at the same time.

▶ Check if bleeding is controlled. Slowly release your fingers from the artery while maintaining direct pressure on the bleeding site. If bleeding increases when pressure is lifted, you have found the right spot.

TOURNIQUETS

- Place a belt or a two-inch-wide band of cloth around the injured extremity and tighten with a windlass (stick or other rigid object) until the blood flow is cut off. (See **HOW TO REMOVE YOUR OWN LIMB** in the next chapter for more information on proper use of a tourniquet and windlass.)

- Place the tourniquet in the midportion of the upper arm or leg. Larger victims may need two tourniquets, especially on the thigh.

- For gunshot and blast wounds, place the tourniquet as high on the arm or leg as possible, since bullet or shrapnel fragments can migrate up the arm or leg, away from the entry point.

3 **Immobilize the injured area.**

Use a splint to immobilize the extremity and protect it from further injury, and to maintain the clotting process.

4 **Dress the wound.**

Gently irrigate the injury with clean water, and then dress with clean cloth to prevent infection.

If available, a hemostatic powder or dressing (HemCon, QuickClot, Combat Gauze) will encourage blood clotting. Continue to apply pressure to the wound for five minutes after applying the hemostatic agent.

IF THE WOUND IS TO THE CHEST

Open chest wounds—also called "sucking" chest wounds, because inhaled air enters the wound instead of the trachea, resulting in a sucking sound—usually occur from high-velocity projectiles that enter the chest and leave a hole nearly the same size as the trachea (wind pipe). If the chest is not sealed, the victim will suffocate.

1 **Dry the area around the wound.**

Tape will not stick to moist or blood-covered skin.

2 **Wait for the victim to exhale.**

Sealing the chest before the victim exhales may trap air in the space surrounding the lung and make breathing difficult.

3 **Wrap the victim's chest.**

Use any airtight (occlusive) plastic material such as plastic wrap, a large plastic bag, or other airtight fabric to seal the wound. Secure the plastic on three sides with tape, allowing any air and blood to drain from the open side of the dressing.

4 **Monitor the victim's breathing.**

If breathing becomes more labored, lift the dressing to release the air.

PRO TIP

During transport, roll the victim onto the injured side to allow blood to drain and the uninjured lung to breathe.

CHAPTER SEVEN

Adventure Survival

HOW TO ESCAPE FROM QUICKSAND

1 **Stay calm.**

Quicksand is dense, and you are more buoyant in quicksand than you are in water; floating is relatively easy.

2 **Do not struggle.**

Remain vertical until you sink to your knees.

3 **As gently as possible, flop slowly onto your back.**

Keep your thighs and upper body horizontal and parallel to the ground.

4 **Once you are stable, pull your lower legs out of the quicksand first.**

This will be difficult: quicksand is about twice as dense as water. Move slowly and deliberately.

5 **Roll to safety.**

Once your legs are free, roll on top of the quicksand toward solid ground. If a tree branch or root is within reach, grab it and use that to pull you out, again moving slowly.

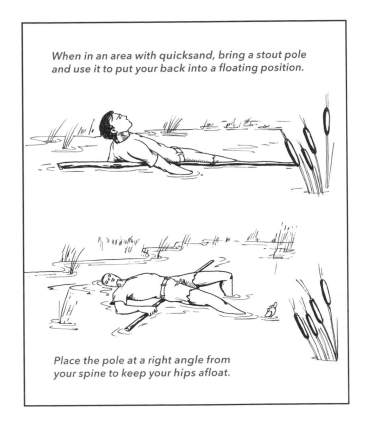

When in an area with quicksand, bring a stout pole and use it to put your back into a floating position.

Place the pole at a right angle from your spine to keep your hips afloat.

WALKING WITH A POLE

When walking in quicksand country, carry a stout pole—roughly the diameter of your wrist and as long as your height. It will help you get out should you need to.

1 **Lay the pole on the surface of the quicksand.**
Do this as soon as you begin to sink.

2   **Gently flop onto your back on top of the pole.**

After a minute or two, equilibrium in the quicksand will be achieved, and you will no longer sink.

3   **Move the pole to rest under your hips and at a right angle to your spine.**

The pole will keep your hips from sinking.

4   **Free your legs.**

Slowly pull out first one leg and then the other.

5   **Roll to safety.**

Take the shortest route to firmer ground, moving slowly.

HOW TO AVOID SINKING

Quicksand is just ordinary sand mixed with upwelling water, which makes it behave like a liquid. However, in order to pull a limb out of quicksand, you have to work against the vacuum left behind.

▶   Move slowly to lower the viscosity of the quicksand, which increases with shearing.

▶   Spread your arms and legs far apart and float on your back. Humans are less dense than fresh water, and salt water is slightly more dense. Floating is easier in salt water than fresh water and much easier in quicksand. The natural "float level" is around your ribs in quicksand, while it's around your neck in fresh water.

HOW TO SURVIVE ADRIFT AT SEA

1 **Stay with your ship until you have to "step up" into your life raft.**

Your best chance of survival is on a boat—even a disabled one—not on a life raft. If the boat is sinking and you cannot pump seawater out, take the following steps.

2 **Remain calm.**

Assuming it was properly registered, your craft's water-activated Emergency Position Indicating Radio Beacon, or 406MHz "EPiRB," will send out a global marine distress signal with your boat's identification and position. (If unregistered, there's a chance emergency response will be delayed or, in some cases, never materialize.)

3 **Grab your "go-bag."**

Your prepacked go-bag should be within reach of the companionway and should contain the following:

- ▸ A waterproof handheld VHF (very high frequency) radio to communicate with passing ships and rescuers

- ▸ Warm, dry clothes, a hat, and space blankets
- ▸ Food (dried fruits/nuts/granola or protein bars)
- ▸ A small, handheld GPS tracking unit
- ▸ Drinking water in portable jugs (as many as you can carry)
- ▸ A compass
- ▸ A flashlight with extra batteries
- ▸ Handheld flares
- ▸ A handheld water-maker

4 **Prepare to board the life raft.**

Securely tie the life raft to the boat before pulling the inflation cord. Once aboard the raft, cut the line.

5 **Activate your Personal Locator Beacon (PLB).**

PLBs also rely on the 406MHz satellite signal, and they are small enough to be worn. These units can also have GPS accuracy, but battery life is required to transmit for only 24 hours, so you could be without GPS after that. PLBs are not water-activated in an overboard emergency and do not offer the safety features of full-size 406 EPiRBs.

6 **Do not drink seawater.**

A person can last for days or even weeks at sea without food, but without clean water to drink, death is a virtual certainty within several days.

- ▶ If worse comes to worst, throw extra jugs of water overboard from the disabled boat so that you can retrieve them later—they will float. Tether them to your life raft, so they don't float away.

- ▶ Many canned foods, particularly vegetables, are packed in water, so take those with you if you can.

- ▶ Do not ration water; drink it as needed, but don't drink more than is necessary—a half-gallon a day should be sufficient if you limit your activity.

7 **Stay warm.**

If you are in a cold water/weather environment, you are more likely to die of exposure or hypothermia than of anything else. Put on dry clothes and stay out of the water. Prolonged exposure to salt water can damage your skin and cause lesions, which are prone to infection.

8 **Stay covered.**

Modern life rafts have canopies, which protect passengers from sun, wind, and rain. If the canopy is missing or damaged, wear a hat, long sleeves, and pants to protect yourself from the sun.

9 **Find food, if you can.**

Life rafts include fishing hooks in their survival kits. If your raft is floating for several weeks, seaweed will form on its underside and fish will naturally congregate in the shade under the raft. You can catch them with the hook and eat the flesh raw. If no hook is available, you can fashion one using wire or even shards of aluminum from an empty can.

10 **Try to get to land, if you know where it is.**

Most rafts include small paddles, but life rafts are not very maneuverable, especially in any wind above three knots. Do not exhaust yourself—you will not be able to move any significant distance without great effort.

11 **If you see a plane or boat nearby, try to signal them.**

Use the VHF radio or a handheld flare kit to get their attention. A small mirror can also be used for signaling.

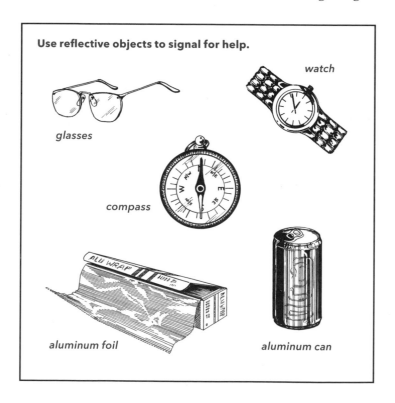

Use reflective objects to signal for help.

watch

glasses

compass

aluminum foil

aluminum can

HOW TO SURVIVE WHEN LOST IN THE DESERT

1 **Do not panic.**

Remain calm, especially if people know where you are and when you are scheduled to return.

2 **If you have a vehicle, stay with it.**

Do not wander.

3 **If you are on foot, try to backtrack by retracing your steps.**

Always move downstream or down country. Travel along ridges instead of in washes or valleys, where it is harder for you to see and for rescuers to see you.

4 **If you have completely lost your bearings, try to get to a high vista and look around.**

If you are not absolutely sure you can follow your tracks or prints, stay put.

5 **Build and maintain signal fires.**

Build smoky fires during daylight hours (tires work well), but keep a bright fire burning at night. If fuel is limited, keep a small kindling-fire burning and have fuel ready to burn if you spot a person or vehicle. To extend the burning time of gasoline, stuff a toilet roll into a tin or can and add gasoline, and then cover with a top to prevent evaporation until ready to use.

6 **Make a "Benghazi burner."**

British WWII soldiers used these burners to make tea as well as for signaling. Fill a can with sand, and then pour gasoline into it, creating a gas-based "mud" that will burn for an extended period of time.

7 **Make a distress signal.**

If a car or plane is passing, or if you see other people off in the distance, try to signal them by making a very large triangle in a clearing using available, ideally reflective, materials. The triangle is the international symbol for distress. Additional signals include the following:

- ▶ **I** indicates to rescuers that someone is injured.

- ▶ **X** means you are unable to proceed.

- ▶ **F** indicates you need food and water.

- ▶ Three shots from a gun is another recognized distress signal.

8 **Rest frequently to avoid heat prostration.**

Desert conditions can exceed 120° Fahrenheit during the day, and shade can be scarce. In the summer, sit at least 12 inches above the ground on a stool or a branch (ground temperatures can be 30 degrees hotter than the surrounding air temperature).

9 **Travel in the evening, at night, or early in the day.**

If you must walk during daylight hours:

- ▶ Walk slowly to conserve energy and rest at least 10 minutes every hour.

- ▶ Drink water; don't ration it.

- ▶ Avoid talking and smoking.

- ▶ Breathe through your nose, not your mouth.

- ▶ Avoid alcohol, which dehydrates.

- ▶ Avoid eating if there is not a sufficient amount of water readily available; digestion consumes water.

- ▶ Stay in the shade and wear clothing, including a shirt, hat, and sunglasses. Clothing helps ration sweat by slowing evaporation and prolonging cooling.

10 **In cold weather, wear layers of clothing.**

Make sure you and your clothes are dry. Watch for signs of hypothermia, which include intense shivering, muscle tensing, fatigue, poor coordination, stumbling, and blueness of the lips and fingernails. If you see these signs, get dry clothing on immediately and light a fire if possible. If not, huddle close to companions for warmth.

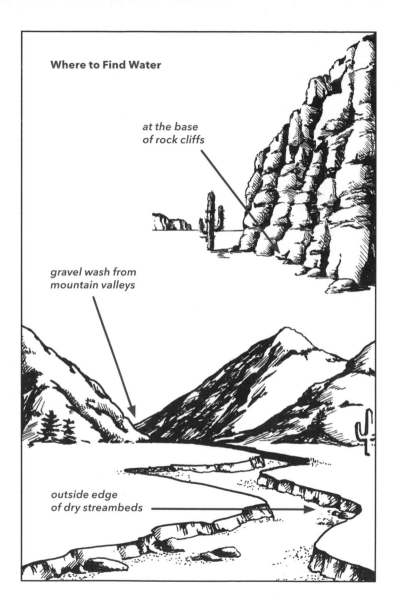

Where to Find Water

at the base
of rock cliffs

gravel wash from
mountain valleys

outside edge
of dry streambeds

near green vegetation

11 **Find water.**

Look for water in likely areas:

▶ The base of rock cliffs.

▶ In the gravel wash from mountain valleys, especially after a recent rain.

▶ The outside edge of a sharp bend in a dry streambed. Look for wet sand, and then dig down three to six feet to find seeping water.

▶ Near green vegetation. Tree clusters and other shrubbery, such as cottonwood, sycamore, or willow trees, may indicate the presence of water.

▶ Animal paths and flocks of birds. Following them may lead you to water.

12 **Eat cactus fruit and flowers.**

Split open the base of cactus stalks and chew on the pith, but don't swallow it. Carry chunks of pith to alleviate thirst while walking. Avoid any cactus that exudes white sap, which is toxic and may burn the mucus membranes of the mouth and throat. Other desert plants are inedible and will make you sick.

Cactus fruit and flowers can be eaten. Split open the base and chew on the pith.

HOW TO PREPARE

When planning a trip to a desert area that is sparsely populated, always inform someone of your destination, the duration of the trip, and its intended route. Otherwise no one will come looking for you if you get lost. If traveling by car, make sure your vehicle is in good condition, and make sure you have the following:

- ▶ A sound battery
- ▶ Good hoses (squeeze them: they should be firm, not soft and mushy)
- ▶ A spare tire with the proper inflation
- ▶ Spare fan belts
- ▶ Tools
- ▶ Reserve gasoline and oil
- ▶ Water (five gallons for a vehicle)

HOW TO DRIVE SAFELY

- ▶ Keep an eye on the sky. Flash floods can occur in a wash any time thunderheads are in sight, even though it may not be raining where you are.
- ▶ If you get caught in a dust storm, get off the road immediately. Turn off your driving lights and turn on your emergency flashers. Back into the wind to reduce windshield pitting by sand particles.

- Before driving through washes and sandy areas, test the footing. One minute on foot may save hours of hard work and prevent a punctured oil pan.

- If your vehicle breaks down, stay near it; your emergency supplies are there. Raise the hood and trunk lid to denote "help needed." A vehicle can be seen for miles, but a person is very difficult to find.

- Leave a disabled vehicle only if you are positive of the route to help.

- If stalled or lost, set signal fires. Set smoky fires in the daytime, bright ones for the night. Three fires in a triangle denote "help needed."

- If you find a road, stay on it.

WHAT TO BRING WHEN TRAVELING BY FOOT

- Water (one gallon per person per day is adequate; two or more gallons is smarter and safer)

- A map that shows the nearest populated areas

- Waterproof matches

- A cigarette lighter or flint and steel

- A survival guide

- Strong sunscreen, a hat, warm clothes, and blankets

- A pocketknife

- A metal signaling mirror

- Iodine tablets
- A small pencil and writing materials
- A whistle (three blasts denote "help needed")
- A canteen cup
- Aluminum foil
- A compass
- A first aid kit

HOW TO AVOID GETTING LOST

- When hiking, periodically look back in the direction from where you have come. Taking a mental picture of what it will look like when you return helps in case you become lost.
- Stay on established trails if possible and mark the trail route with blazes (any sort of directional marks) on trees and brush, or by making *ducques* (pronounced "ducks"), piles of three rocks stacked on top of one another.

HOW TO SURVIVE WHEN LOST IN THE MOUNTAINS

The number one cause of death when lost in the mountains is hypothermia—humans are basically tropical animals. Staying calm in the face of darkness, loneliness, and the unknown will greatly increase your chances of survival. Around 80 percent of mountain survival is your reaction to fear, 10 percent is your survival gear, and the other 10 percent is knowing how to use it. Always tell someone else where you are going and when you will return.

1 **Do not panic.**

If you told someone where you were going, search and rescue teams will be looking for you. (In general, teams will search only during daylight hours for adults, but they will search around the clock for children who are alone.)

2 **Find shelter, and stay warm and dry.**

Exerting yourself unnecessarily—like dragging heavy logs to build a shelter—will make you sweat and make you cold. Use the shelter around you before trying to construct one. If you are in a snow-covered area, you may be able to dig

Build a snow cave or trench for shelter and warmth. Use dead leaves and branches for insulation.

a cave in deep snow for shelter and protection from the wind. A snow trench may be a better idea—it requires less exertion. Simply use something to dig a trench, get in it, and cover it with branches or leaves. You should attempt to make your shelter in the middle of the mountain if possible. Stay out of the valleys—cold air falls, and the valley floor can be the coldest spot on the mountain.

3 **Signal rescuers for help.**

The best time to signal rescuers is during the day, with a signaling device or three fires in a triangle. Signal for help from the highest point possible—it will be easier for rescuers to see you, and any sound you make will travel farther. Build three smoky fires and put your blanket—gold side facing out, if it is a space blanket—on the ground.

4 **Do not wander far.**

It will make finding you more difficult, as search teams will be trying to retrace your path and may miss you if you have gone off in a different direction. Searchers often wind up finding a vehicle with no one in it because the driver has wandered off.

5 **If you get frostbite, do not rewarm the affected area until you're out of danger.**

You can walk on frostbitten feet, but once you warm the area and can feel the pain, you will not want to walk anywhere. Try to protect the frostbitten area and keep it dry until you are rescued.

HOW TO PREPARE

You must dress properly before entering a wilderness area. Layer your clothing in the following manner:

FIRST (INNER) LAYER Long underwear, preferably polypropylene. This provides only slight insulation—its purpose is to draw moisture off your skin.

SECOND (MIDDLE) LAYER Something to trap and create warm "dead air" space, such as a down parka.

THIRD (OUTER) LAYER A Gore-Tex or other brand of breathable jacket that allows moisture out but not in. Dry insulation is key to your survival. Once you are wet, it is very difficult to get dry.

Make sure you have the following items in your survival kit, and that you know how to use them (reading the instructions for the first time in the dark wilderness is not recommended):

▶ **A HEAT SOURCE** Bring several boxes of waterproof matches, as well as a lighter. Trioxane—a small, light, chemical heat source that the Army uses—is recommended. Trioxane packs can be picked up in outdoor and military surplus stores. Dryer lint is also highly flammable and very lightweight.

▶ **SHELTER** Carry a small space blanket, which has a foil-like coating that insulates you. Get one that is silver on one side (for warmth) and orange-gold on the other, which can be used for signaling. The silver side is not a good color to signal with. It can be mistaken for ice or mineral rock. The orange-gold color does not occur in nature and will not be mistaken for anything else.

▶ **A SIGNALING DEVICE** A small mirror works well, as do flares or a whistle, which carries much farther than a voice.

▶ **FOOD** Pack carbohydrates: bagels, trail mix, granola bars, and so on. Proteins need heat to break down and require more water for digestion.

HOW TO AVOID BEING STRUCK BY LIGHTNING

No place is completely safe from lightning—a lightning bolt can carry more than 100 million volts of energy. However, some places are more dangerous than others. Four-walled buildings and cars (nonconvertibles) are generally safer places to seek shelter during a thunderstorm.

1 **Beware of loud or frequent thunder.**

If you can see lightning and/or hear thunder, you are at risk. High winds, rainfall, and cloud cover often act as precursors to actual cloud-to-ground strikes. Thunderstorms generally move west to east and occur late in the day or in early evening when humidity is highest.

2 **Count the time between seeing lightning and hearing thunder.**

Count the number of seconds between lightning and thunder and divide by five. This will indicate how far the storm is from you, in miles. (Sound travels at 1,100 feet per second.) However, be aware that in an active thunderstorm there may be multiple lightning flashes in a short amount of time, making it difficult to accurately pair a flash with a given boom of thunder. When in doubt, remember "when thunder roars, go indoors."

3 **Use the "30:30" rule when assessing lightning danger.**

If the time delay between seeing the flash (lightning) and hearing the boom (thunder) is fewer than 30 seconds, seek a safer location immediately. Wait 30 minutes from the last thunder before leaving your shelter.

4 **Beware of higher risk situations.**

- ▸ Avoid high places, open fields, and ridges above the timberline.

- ▸ Avoid isolated trees, unprotected gazebos, and rain or picnic shelters, as well as shallow depressions in the earth—current traveling through the ground may use you to bridge the depression.

- ▸ Avoid communications towers, flagpoles, light poles, metal and wood bleachers, and metal fences.

- ▸ Avoid bodies of water: oceans, lakes, swimming pools, and rivers.

- ▸ Avoid golf carts and convertibles.

- ▸ If you are camping, avoid your tent if it is in an open area or under a large tree.

- ▸ If you are on a technical climb, sit on your rope or backpack—anything that is not metallic. Tie off your belay; this will anchor you if a strike occurs and you are knocked off-balance.

5 **If you get caught in an open area during a storm, assume the "lightning position."**

Crouch into a squat, making yourself as small as possible, and cover your ears. Do not lie flat on the ground, which would increase your chances of being hit by ground current.

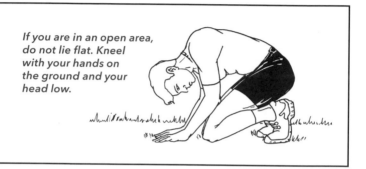

If you are in an open area, do not lie flat. Kneel with your hands on the ground and your head low.

6 **Wait for the storm to pass.**

The lightning threat generally diminishes with time after the last sound of thunder, but may persist for more than 30 minutes. When thunderstorms are in the area but not overhead, the lightning threat can exist even when it is sunny, not raining, or when clear sky is visible.

PRO TIPS

▶ Large enclosed buildings tend to be much safer than smaller or open structures. The risk for lightning injury depends on whether the structure incorporates lightning protection, the construction materials used, and the size of the structure.

DO NOT
stand under a tree.

- ▶ Fully enclosed metal vehicles such as cars, trucks, buses, vans, and fully enclosed farm vehicles with the windows rolled up provide good shelter from lightning. Avoid contact with metal or conducting surfaces outside or inside the vehicle.

- ▶ When inside, avoid contact with conductive surfaces with exposure to the outside, including the shower, sink, plumbing fixtures, and metal door and window frames.

- ▶ Avoid outlets, electrical cords, and wired electrical devices, including telephones, computers, and televisions (particularly cable TVs).

HOW TO TREAT SOMEONE STRUCK BY LIGHTNING

1 **Call to report the strike and give directions to emergency personnel.**

With immediate medical treatment, victims can survive an encounter with lightning. If multiple people have been struck, treat the apparently "dead" first. People who are unconscious but still breathing will probably recover on their own. Common injuries include ruptured eardrums, loss of consciousness, and a unique paralysis called keraunoparalysis, where a victim's arm or leg will become pale and immobile. This paralysis will resolve on its own within several hours.

2 **Move to a safer location to avoid getting struck yourself.**

It is unusual for victims who survive a lightning strike to have major fractures that would cause paralysis or major bleeding complications unless they have suffered a fall or been thrown a distance. Do not be afraid to move the victim rapidly if necessary; individuals struck by lightning do not carry a charge and it is safe to touch them to give medical treatment.

3 **In cold and wet environments, put a protective layer between the victim and the ground.**

This will decrease the chance of hypothermia, which can further complicate resuscitation.

4   Check for burns, especially around jewelry and watches.

Remove jewelry or watches before more swelling sets in.

5   If the victim is not breathing, start mouth-to-mouth resuscitation.

Give one breath every five seconds. If moving the victim, give a few quick breaths prior to moving.

6   Determine if the victim has a pulse.

Check the pulse at the carotid artery (side of the neck) or femoral artery (groin) for at least 20 to 30 seconds.

7   If no pulse is detected, start cardiac compressions.

8   If the pulse returns, continue ventilation with rescue breathing.

Continue as needed for as long as practical in a wilderness situation.

9   If a pulse does not return after 20 to 30 minutes of good effort, stop resuscitation efforts.

In wilderness areas far from medical care, prolonged basic CPR is of little use—the victim is unlikely to recover if they do not respond within the first few minutes.

HOW TO REMOVE YOUR OWN LIMB

WHAT YOU WILL NEED

▶ A sharp pocketknife or cutting tool, ideally with an additional sawtooth blade

▶ A tourniquet (leather belt or two-inch-wide strip of cloth)

▶ A windlass (stout rod or stick to tighten the tourniquet)

1 **Numb the area of entrapment (optional).**

If ice, snow, or cold water is available, cover or immerse the area of the limb closest to the point of entrapment until thoroughly numb or completely frostbitten. Perform this step only if amputation is the only option.

2 **Position the tourniquet.**

Loosely wrap the tourniquet around a single bone. If a leg or foot is entrapped, place it on the thigh just above the knee. If an arm or hand is entrapped, place it on the upper arm above the elbow, not on the forearm. If the bone is already broken, position it just above the break. Tie off.

3   **Tighten.**

Insert the windlass over the tourniquet, tie loose ends in a knot over the windlass, and turn the windlass until extremely tight. If there is no capillary refill (the pressed area remains white), it is sufficiently tight. Tie another knot over the windlass to secure in position.

4   **Prep for surgery.**

Keep a dry cloth at hand to clear the amputation site of seeping blood. The tourniquet should reduce bleeding to manageable levels.

5   **Protect your head.**

You will probably pass out from the pain, coming to within about 30 seconds. Keep your head away from rocks or other objects that may cause injury when you fall unconscious.

6   **Begin cutting.**

If the bone is broken, cut at the break. Otherwise, begin amputation at the joint closest to the area of entrapment: elbow, wrist, knee, or ankle. Feel for the depression just below the bone and use the knife to cut skin and tissue. Make sharp, deep cuts; do not use a sawing motion. Keep the area clear of blood using the cloth. Push tissue back and away from the cut so your view is unobstructed. If you pass out, proceed after coming to. Once you reach the bone, the sawtoothed blade may be helpful. You should be able to completely sever a limb in 10–15 minutes.

7 **Remove the entrapped limb.**

Once you have cut through the joint, loosen the entrapped limb and pull free. Place a second tourniquet directly above the amputation site and tighten. Remove the first tourniquet.

8 **Pad the stump using cloth strips and clothing, and seek medical assistance.**

PRO TIP

▶ Traumatic amputation of a limb is not necessarily a fatal injury. In order of severity, the immediate problems that you must deal with are rapid severe arterial bleeding; slower bleeding from cut veins; pain; and infection. Only severe bleeding carries an immediate, life-threatening risk, with the possibility of death in minutes.

HOW TO SURVIVE
AN AVALANCHE

1 **Stay on top of the snow.**

Struggle to stay on top of the snow by using a freestyle swimming motion. If this fails, cross your arm over your face with a bent elbow—this will keep the snow from plugging your mouth and nose, and may help form an air pocket.

2 **If partially buried, wave and kick to dig free.**

Use your arms and legs to dig free of the snow, if possible. The snow in an avalanche is like a wet snowball or even cement: it is not light and powdery, and once you are buried, it is very difficult to dig your way out.

3 **If completely buried, probe for direction, and dig.**

If you are buried, your best chance of survival is if someone saw you get covered. However, if you still have a ski pole, poke through the snow in several directions until you see or feel open air, then dig in that direction. Otherwise, dig a small hole around you and spit in it. The saliva should head downhill, giving you an idea of which direction is up. Dig up, and do it quickly.

Struggle to stay on top of the snow by using a freestyle swimming motion.

WHAT TO BRING WHEN TRAVELING IN AVALANCHE COUNTRY

▸ **AN AVALANCHE BEACON** This broadcasts your position by setting up a magnetic field that can be picked up by the other beacons in your group.

▸ **AN AVALANCHE PROBE** These are sturdy, sectional aluminum poles that fit together to create a probe six to eight feet in length. Some ski poles are threaded and can be screwed together to form avalanche probes.

- ▶ **A SMALL, COLLAPSIBLE METAL SHOVEL** Plastic shovels are not strong enough to dig through densely packed avalanche snow.

- ▶ **AN AIRBAG** These devices are worn like a backpack and can be inflated using a ripcord in the event of an avalanche, helping you float above the snow.

PRO TIPS

- ▶ Never go hiking or skiing alone in avalanche territory.

- ▶ Avalanches occur in areas with new snow; on the leeward side of mountains (facing away from the wind); and in the afternoons of sunny days, when the morning sun may have loosened the snowpack. They occur most often on mountainsides with angles of 30-45 degrees, which are often the most popular slopes for skiing.

- ▶ Avalanches can be triggered by numerous factors, including recent snowfall, wind, and sunlight. As new snow accumulates with successive storms, the layers may be of different consistencies and may not bind to one another, making the snow highly unstable.

- ▶ Loud noises do not cause avalanches, unless they cause significant vibrations in the ground or snow.

- ▶ The activity with the highest avalanche risk is now snow-mobiling, because the light and powerful vehicles can get high into mountainous terrain, where avalanches occur.

- ▶ If skiing with others on a dangerous slope, go down one at a time, not as a group, in case a slide occurs.

HOW TO RESCUE OTHERS

1 **Get help.**

If you have witnessed others being buried by an avalanche, contact local search and rescue groups as soon as possible; ski patrol will not be available in the backcountry.

2 **Act quickly.**

Chances of survival are less than 50 percent if victims are not found and uncovered within 30 minutes.

3 **Look for clothing or gear on top of the snow surface.**

This may indicate that victims are nearby. If you have a beacon, switch it into "search mode" and use a zigzag pattern to look for a signal.

4 **Use your avalanche probe.**

Once you've located a strong signal, use your avalanche probe to feel under the snow for a victim.

5 **Use a collapsible shovel to dig out the victim.**

HOW TO SURVIVE IF YOUR PARACHUTE FAILS TO OPEN

WITH A JUMPING PARTNER

1 **Signal a jumping partner immediately.**

Skydivers generally deploy their parachutes 15 to 20 seconds above the ground, so you'll have to act quickly. As soon as you realize that your chute is bad, signal to a jumping companion whose chute has not yet opened that you are having a malfunction. Wave your arms and point to your chute.

2 **When your companion (and new best friend) gets to you, hook arms.**

3 **Secure your grip.**

When your friend opens his chute, you will be falling at terminal velocity—about 130 miles per hour, with G forces tripling or quadrupling your body weight—and there will be no way either of you can hold on to one another

Hook arms with your companion. Then hook your arms into their chest strap, up to the elbows, and grab hold of your own.

normally. Hook your arms into his chest strap, or through the two sides of the front of his harness, all the way up to your elbows, and grab hold of your own strap.

4 **Open the chute.**

The chute opening shock will be severe, probably enough to dislocate or break your arms.

5 **Steer the canopy.**

Your friend must now hold on to you with one arm while steering his canopy (the part of the chute that controls direction and speed). If the canopy is slow and big, you may hit the ground slowly enough to break only a leg, and your chances of survival are high. If the canopy is fast, your friend will have to maneuver to avoid hitting the ground too fast. You must also avoid power lines and other obstructions at all costs.

6 **Aim for a body of water.**

If there is a body of water nearby, head for that. Note however that once you hit the water, you will have to tread with just your legs and hope that your partner is able to pull you out before the chute takes in water.

IF NO ONE CAN REACH YOU

If you are on your own and have a double chute malfunction—or a "nothing out"—all is not lost.

1 **Grab your hook knife and make a small slit in the elastic pouch that holds the pilot chute, which deploys the main chute.**

A small slit of an inch or less in the chute pouch may allow the pilot chute to be extracted and released into the airstream, automatically inflating the main parachute.

2 **If this does not work and you are still free-falling, aim for terrain to break your fall.**

Aim for trees or a swampy area with some canopy/ tree cover, as tree branches and undergrowth may slow your descent and break your fall slightly. If no trees are available, land on sloped, not flat, terrain.

3 **Land on your back.**

Your nondeployed parachute may provide some added cushioning and protection. Fold your body into a "V" as you land, and protect your head with your hands.

HOW TO PREPARE

Check your chute before you jump. The good news is that today's parachutes are built to open, so even if you make big mistakes packing them, they tend to sort themselves out. The reserve chute, however, must be packed by a certified rigger and must be perfect as it is your last resort. Make sure that:

▶ the parachute is folded in straight lines—that there are no twists and the slider is positioned correctly to keep the parachute from opening too fast.

HOW TO GET TO THE SURFACE IF YOUR SCUBA TANK RUNS OUT OF AIR

1   Do not panic.

2   Signal to your fellow divers that you are having a problem.

Point to your tank or regulator.

3   Share a regulator, passing it back and forth while swimming slowly to the surface.

Take two breaths, and then pass it back to the other diver. Ascend together, exhaling as you go. Then take another two breaths, alternating, until you reach the surface. Nearly all divers carry an extra regulator connected to their tank.

4   If no one can help you, keep your regulator in your mouth.

Air may expand in the tank as you ascend, giving you additional breaths.

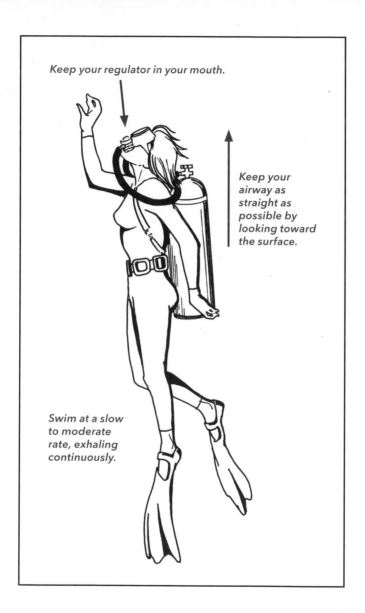

Keep your regulator in your mouth.

Keep your airway as straight as possible by looking toward the surface.

Swim at a slow to moderate rate, exhaling continuously.

5 **Look straight up so that your airway is as straight as possible.**

Swim to the surface at a slow to moderate rate.

6 **Exhale slowly and continuously as you swim up.**

It is very important that you exhale the entire way up— if you do not exhale continuously, you risk an embolism— but the rate at which you exhale is also important. Exhale slowly. Do not exhaust all your air in the first few seconds of your ascent. As long as you are even slightly exhaling, your passageway will be open and air can vent from your lungs.

PRO TIPS

- Never dive alone.

- Watch your pressure and depth gauges closely.

- Make sure your fellow divers are within easy signaling and swimming distance.

- Share a regulator in an emergency. It is much safer to use your partner's regulator than to try to make a quick swim to the surface. This is especially true the deeper you are, where you need to surface gradually.

- Always use an alternate air source instead of swimming up, unless you are fewer than 30 feet below the surface.

HOW TO MAKE FIRE WITHOUT MATCHES

WHAT YOU WILL NEED

- ▶ **KNIFE**

- ▶ **KINDLING** Several pieces, varying in size from small to large.

- ▶ **WOOD** Any dry wood will work to keep the fire going. Hold the wood against your bottom lip. If it feels cool it is probably wet; if it feels warm after a second or two, it is dry enough to use.

- ▶ **BOW** A curved stick as long as your arm from armpit to fingertip, about two feet.

- ▶ **STRING** A shoelace, parachute cord, or leather thong. If using parachute cord, remove the inner strands, which will give it a tighter grip on the spindle. Primitive cordage can be made from yucca, milkweed, or another tough, stringy plant.

- ▶ **SOCKET** A horn, bone, piece of hardwood, rock, or seashell that fits in the palm of the hand and will be placed over a stick.

- ▶ **LUBE** You can use earwax, skin oil, a ball of green grass, lip balm, or anything else oily.

- ▶ **SPINDLE** A dry, straight ¾-to-1-inch-diameter stick approximately 8–10 inches long. The wood should be soft enough so your thumbnail easily leaves an indent when pushed into it. Round one end and carve the other end to a point.

- ▶ **FIRE BOARD** Select and shape a second piece of wood into a board approximately ¾–1 inch thick, 2–3 inches wide, and 10–12 inches long. As mentioned earlier, the wood should be soft enough to imprint with your thumbnail. The wood grain should be on a vertical perspective (running from bottom to top). Carve a shallow dish in the center of the flat side approximately ½ inch from the edge. Then cut a triangular-shaped notch into the dish with the triangle's wide base facing out and point facing inward to the center of the dish.

- ▶ **TRAY** A piece of bark, deadwood, or leaf inserted under the V-shaped notch to catch the ember. A small, flat piece of carved bone can also be used.

- ▶ **NEST** Dry bark, grass, leaves, cattail fuzz, or some other combustible material, formed into a bird's nest shape.

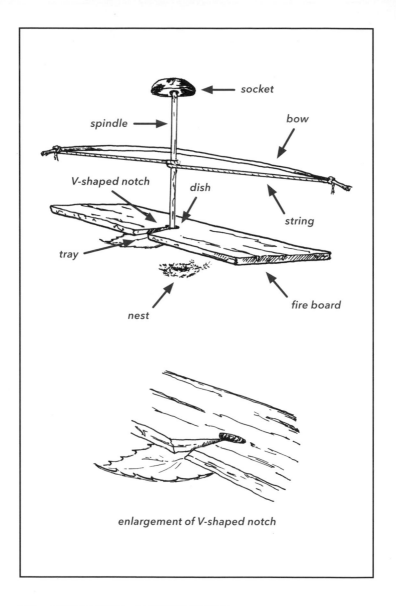

socket

spindle

bow

V-shaped notch

dish

string

tray

nest

fire board

enlargement of V-shaped notch

How to Start the Fire

1 **Tie the string tightly to the bow.**

Tie one end to each end of the stick.

2 **Secure the board.**

Kneel on your right knee, with the ball of your left foot on the fire board, holding it firmly to the ground.

3 **Set the tray below the notch of the board.**

4 **Take the bow in your hands.**

5 **Loop the string in the center of the bow.**

6 **Insert the spindle in the loop of the bowstring.**

Insert the spindle so that it is on the inside of the string of the bow, pointed end up. The bowstring should now be tight—if not, loop the string around the spindle a few more times, or tighten the string at one end. Place the thumb of the hand holding the bow onto the string so you can apply extra pressure to it if needed.

7 **Lubricate the hand socket.**

Take the hand socket in your left hand, notch side down, and lubricate the notch.

8 **Place the rounded end of the spindle into the dish of the board and the pointed end of the spindle into the hand socket.**

9 Pressing down lightly on the socket, draw the bow back and forth.

This will rotate the spindle slowly. Draw the bow slowly back and forth using its full length.

10 Add pressure to the socket and speed to your bowing.

As the wood heats up, add more pressure bearing down on the socket. Look down into the notch. You should see dust building in the notch that will start to smoke. Apply more speed and pressure. When you see a large amount of smoke coming from the notch, you have created a fire ember.

11 Stop bowing.

Set aside the spindle.

12 Preserve the ember.

Hold the ember in place on the tray with a leaf or small-pointed stick, remove the board and set it aside. Gently wave your hand or a hat over the ember to encourage airflow until it glows. Do not blow on the ember: you may blow it away, or the moisture from your breath may put it out.

13 Remove the tray and transfer the ember into your "nest."

Tie a string tightly
to the bow.

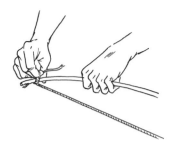

Loop the string in the center
and insert the spindle.

Press down lightly on
the socket. Draw the
bow back and forth,
rotating the spindle.

14 **Hold the nest tightly and wave steadily over the ember.**

Eventually, the nest will catch fire.

15 **Add kindling onto the nest.**

When the kindling catches, gradually add larger pieces of fuel.

PRO TIPS

▶ You should not be dependent on any primitive fire method to maintain life in a wilderness survival emergency.

▶ Making fire in this manner can be quite difficult under harsh conditions (rain, snow, cold).

▶ Practice this method at home to familiarize yourself with the quirks of the process.

HOW TO SURVIVE DEHYDRATION

1 **Conserve water, but drink it.**

If you have water, even a small amount, don't save it—drink it. Roughly divide the total amount into four to six portions and drink one portion every few hours as needed.

2 **Limit food intake.**

Proper digestion requires liquid. However, if sufficient food is available, eat small amounts to maintain your strength.

3 **Limit movement to evening and nighttime.**

Dry desert areas may be hot during the day but very cool at night. Perspiration exacerbates dehydration, so move only when the air is cool enough to prevent sweating.

4 **Locate gulches or arroyos.**

Desert washes and dry streambeds (arroyos), while appearing parched on the surface, may hold some liquid from previous rains. Locate the outside edge in a sharp turn, and dig at least three feet down. Filter any water through a cloth before drinking. (See **HOW TO SURVIVE WHEN LOST IN THE DESERT** for more information.)

5 Find green vegetation.

Green vegetation draws water from below the surface. Dig below the base of desert plants to find water.

6 Cut cacti.

Using a sharp knife, cut sections from the base of cacti (not the tips or ears). Remove spines, then chew the pith inside, but don't swallow it. Avoid cacti with white sap, and other desert plants.

7 Watch the skies.

Birds require water and may lead you to drinkable sources. Observe where they congregate and search the area for water. If liquid is visible in rock cracks or crevasses, stuff a cloth into the gap, soak up the water, and then wring it into your mouth.

HOW TO PURIFY WATER

There are six primary methods to obtain safe drinking water in the wilderness: filtration, sedimentation, chemical treatment, distillation, boiling, and UV treatment (sunlight). Some methods require two steps before the water is safe to drink.

FILTRATION

Filter water from all sources in the wild: mountain streams, springs, rivers, lakes, or ponds.

1 **Find or make your filter.**

Coffee filters, paper towels, ordinary typing paper, or even your clothing can serve as filters (the more tightly woven, the better). You can also make an effective filter by filling a sock with alternating layers of crushed charcoal, small crushed rocks, and sand.

2 **Pour the water through the filter.**

Do this several times to clean out impurities.

PRO TIP

Filtration will only remove some of the water's impurities. It will not kill bacteria or other microorganisms. The best procedure is to filter water first, then treat it with chemicals, boil it, or expose it to UV light.

SEDIMENTATION

This method will eliminate larger particles in water, but the process takes time and, like filtration, requires a second step to kill microorganisms.

1 **Collect water and leave undisturbed.**

Collect water in clean buckets, bags, or water bottles, and then leave it sitting undisturbed for as long as possible; up to 18 hours may be needed depending on the nature of the sediment.

2 **Remove cleaner water near the surface.**

Once all floating bits settle at the bottom of the container, carefully scoop or pour out the clearer, particulate-free water near the surface.

3 **Purify using boiling, chemical treatment, or UV exposure.**

CHEMICAL TREATMENT

1 **Use bleach or iodine.**

Add two drops of household bleach for each quart of water; use three drops if the water is extremely cold or cloudy. Or use one iodine tablet or five drops of drugstore iodine (2 percent) per quart of water.

2 **Mix the water and bleach or iodine, and let it sit for at least one hour.**

The chemicals will kill microorganisms; the longer the water sits, the purer it will be. Leaving the water overnight is the safest course of action.

DISTILLATION

A solar still uses the heat of the sun to evaporate water trapped in the ground and funnels it into a clean container for drinking. To build a solar still:

1 **Dig a hole about a foot deep.**

Make sure it is wide enough to hold your container.

2 **Place your container at the center of the hole.**

3 **Cover the hole with a piece of plastic.**

A tarp or a section of a garbage bag works well as a cover.

4   Secure the cover.

Place sticks or stones around the edges of the plastic so that it is flush with the ground and air cannot escape.

5   Poke a one-quarter-inch to one-half-inch hole in the center of the tarp.

Place a small stone next to the hole, so the tarp looks like a funnel. Make sure the hole is above, but not touching, the top of the container.

6   Wait.

The heat from the sun will cause water in the ground to evaporate, condense on the plastic, and drip into the container. While your solar still will not produce much liquid (likely less than one cup), the water is safe to drink immediately. The process can take anywhere from several hours to a full day to produce water, depending on the water in the ground and the strength of the sun.

BOILING

Boil water for at least one minute; add one minute for every 3,280 feet of elevation above sea level.

▸   If fuel is abundant, boil water for 10 minutes before drinking it. The longer the water boils, the more microorganisms that are killed. Beyond 10 minutes, however, no further purification occurs. Be sure to let the water cool before drinking it.

▶ If your fuel is limited, be aware that water will be pasteurized and safe to drink (once cool) if it reaches a boil and cools to at least 149° Fahrenheit for six minutes. This will kill all germs, parasites, and viruses. This method saves fuel by limiting unnecessary, lengthy boiling. If the water has fine particulate matter in it due to poor filtration, boil it for two minutes. If it has larger particulate matter, boil for four minutes.

UV TREATMENT

Ultraviolet light from the sun will kill most micro-organisms, and this method can be used once the water is free of sediment.

1 **Pour filtered water into a clear plastic water bottle or bag.**

For highest efficiency, the bag should be no bigger than about one-half gallon (two liters).

2 **Place in bright sunlight for at least six hours.**

EXPERTS AND SOURCES

Chris Ahrens is the Producer of the YouTube channel Lockpicking Heaven's Gate. www.youtube.com/c/chrisahrenslhg

Marcel Altenburg, a Captain in the British armed forces for more than a decade, served in the infantry, the specialized infantry, and as commander of a tank unit. He is a Fellow in Crowd Safety and Risk Analysis at Manchester Metropolitan University in the U.K.

The Arizona State Association of 4 Wheel Drive Clubs

Philip Baum is Managing Director of Green Light Ltd, a U.K. security consultancy for the airline industry; Editor in Chief of *Aviation Security International*; and the author of *Violence in the Skies: A History of Aircraft Hijacking and Bombing.* www.avsec.com

Rich Berkey, MD, has served as an emergency physician in a Level 1 Trauma Center in Portland, Oregon, for more than 20 years.

Jeff Bigham, a Google Scholar, is Associate Professor and Doctoral Program Director at the Human Computer Interaction Institute and the Language Technologies Institute at Carnegie Mellon University's School of Computer Science. www.jeffreybigham.com

Bob Brown, Second Unit Director, is a former stuntman and stunt coordinator, high falls expert, and professional high diver and gymnast. www.brandxstunts.org

Kurt Buhlmann, PhD, Senior Research Associate at the University of Georgia's Savannah River Ecology Laboratory, is a conservation ecologist who focuses on the recovery of rare and endangered amphibians and reptiles.

Bret Butler, a Research Mechanical Engineer with the U.S. Forest Service, studies forest fires with an emphasis on public and firefighter safety. www.firelab.org

Chris Caso, a former stuntman and member of the U.S. gymnastics team, has produced and performed high-fall stunts for numerous movies, including *Batman and Robin, Batman Forever, The Lost World,* and *The Crow: City of Angels.*

Centers for Disease Control and Prevention

Coleman Cooney is Director of the California Academy of Tauromaquia ("The Bullfight School"). www.bullfightschool.com

Richard G. Coss, a retired Professor of Psychology at the University of California, Davis, has studied predator-prey interactions in a variety of species for 40 years, with a focus on predator detection and recognition.

Jim Darlington is a Curator of Reptiles at the St. Augustine Alligator Farm and Zoological Park in Florida. www.alligatorfarm.com.

Chris Davis, MD, DTMH, is Medical Director, Virtual Health-UCHealth, and Assistant Professor in the department of Emergency Medicine at the University of Colorado School of Medicine.

Bella DePaulo, author of *The Psychology of Lying and Detecting Lies*, has written about deception in the *New York Times*, the *Washington Post*, and numerous books and scholarly articles. She teaches at the University of California, Santa Barbara. www.belladepaulo.com

The Desert Survival Guide, a publication of the City of Phoenix, Arizona.

"Mountain" Mel Deweese served as a military Survival Evasion Resistance Escape (SERE) instructor and has taught wilderness survival skills for 30 years. www.youwillsurvive.com

Graham Dickson, Professional Association of Diving Instructors (PADI) master scuba instructor, is President of Arctic Kingdom, an adventure diving company based in Toronto and Iqaluit, Canada.

Mike Donlin is Program Supervisor for Washington state's School Safety Center and speaks to both adults and kids on the dangers of and responses to online and offline dangers in school settings. www.k12.wa.us/SafetyCenter

The Federal Emergency Management Agency

Anna Feigenbaum, PhD, is the author of *Tear Gas: From the Battlefields of World War I to the Streets of Today,* and is Principal Academic in Digital Storytelling at Bournemouth University in the U.K. www.annafeigenbaum.com.

Craig Ferreira, a former Director of the South African White Shark Research Institute, founded White Shark Africa. A White Shark specialist with a particular interest in complex shark behavior, he is the author of *The Shark*, *Great White Sharks on Their Best Behavior,* and *The Submarine.*

Jim Frankenfield is Director of the Cyberspace Snow and Avalanche Center, a nonprofit organization dedicated to avalanche safety education and information, based in Corvallis, Oregon.

Michael G. Frodl, Esq., has been an advisor on maritime piracy risks to the global underwriting and shipping industries for a decade, with a focus on Somalia, Nigeria, Southeast Asia, and the Caribbean. www.c-level.us.com

Brady Geril served as a supervising officer and undercover agent in the New York Police Department's narcotics division for 10 years.

Dale Gibson, a stuntman and stunt coordinator, has appeared in hundreds of commercials and movies.

Bill Hargrove is a licensed locksmith in Pennsylvania with 10 years of experience opening locks.

Troy Hartman is one of the world's foremost skydivers, a pioneer of snowboard-based "skysurfing," and 1997 skysurfing world champion at the X Games. He is currently finalizing design work on a personal jetpack.

Dr. Jeffrey Heit, MD, is a hospitalist at a Boston-area hospital.

John Henkel is Communications Manager for the U.S. Food and Drug Administration and a former contributor to *FDA Consumer* magazine.

Herb Hoelter, CEO & Co-Founder of the National Center on Institutions and Alternatives, is one of the U.S.'s leading experts on inmate sentencing, the federal prison system, and developing alternative programs to incarceration. He has visited more than 300 prisons and counseled thousands of inmates (including Bernie Madoff).

Dave Holder, one of North America's foremost outdoorsmen, has spent two decades in the British military and is a wilderness guide, TV survival consultant, and Canadian Red Cross Wilderness First Aid Instructor. He taught survival tactics to the British and Canadian militaries in the Canadian Rockies for nearly a decade. www.mahikan.ca; www.citylab.com

The Honey Bee Research section of the Agricultural Research Service of the United States Department of Agriculture

Juan Horillo, PhD, is an Associate Professor of Ocean Engineering at the College of Engineering, Texas A&M University, where he develops numerical tools for tsunami calculation.

Andrew P. Jenkins, PhD, WEMT, is a Professor Emeritus of Community Health and Physical Education at Central Washington University and is trained in exercise physiology, wilderness emergency medicine, and mountain rescue.

Joe Jennings, skydiving cinematographer and skydiving coordination specialist, has designed, coordinated, and filmed skydiving stunts for numerous movies, including *Charlie's Angels*, *Triple XXX,* and *Air Force One.*

Kim Kahana is a legendary stuntman who has appeared in more than 300 films, including *Lethal Weapon 3*, *Passenger 57*, and *Smokey and the Bandit.*

Andrew Karam, is a health physicist, board-certified radiation safety expert, and author who specializes in radiological terrorism and the management of radioactive materials programs. He has consulted for the International Atomic Energy Agency and Interpol, among many other organizations. www.andrewkaram.com

Matthew Kennedy is Executive Director of Boxing Ontario, the governing body for Olympic-Style Boxing in Ontario, Canada. www.boxingontario.com

Hubie Kerns, a second-generation stuntman and precision driving instructor, is the owner of Drivers Inc., Hollywood's premiere performance driving school. He has appeared in hundreds of commercials and movies, including *The Fast and the Furious*, *Rush Hour*, and *Jaws*. www.driversinc.com

Dr. Benjamin Kilham is a wildlife biologist and author of *Among the Bears: Raising Orphaned Cubs in the Wild* and *In the Company of Bears: What Bears Have Taught Me About Intelligence and Intuition.*

Cappy Kotz is a USA Boxing certified coach and instructor, and author of *Boxing for Everyone.*

Karl S. Kruszelnicki, Julius Sumner Miller Fellow at the School of Physics of the University of Sydney, Australia, is the author of 43 books. His latest is *Karl, The Universe and Everything.*

The Lightning Safety Group of the American Meteorological Society

John Lindner is Director of the Wilderness Survival School for the Denver group of the Colorado Mountain Club, and retired Director of the Snow Survival School at Safety-One Training, an organization that teaches mountain survival courses to utilities and government agencies.

Grant S. Lipman, MD, FACEP, is a Clinical Associate Professor of Emergency Medicine at Stanford University and Director of the Stanford Wilderness Medicine Section & Fellowship.

David M. Lowell is a certified Master Locksmith and former Education/Proficiency Registration Program Manager of the Associated Locksmiths of America, an industry trade group.

Paul Markowski, Professor of Meteorology at Penn State University, studies tornadogenesis and the forecasting of supercells and tornadoes, and is co-author of *Mesoscale Meteorology in Midlatitudes*, a textbook used worldwide.

Arthur Holland Michel is Co-Director of Bard College's Center for the Study of the Drone, an interdisciplinary research center that examines unmanned systems technologies in military and civilian life. He is working on a book about aerial surveillance technology. www.dronecenter.bard.edu

Vinny Minchillo is a Texas-based car racer, former demolition derby driver, ad guy, typewriter collector, and author of the comedic novel *Spare Me*. www.glasshousestrategy.com

Minnesota Department of Natural Resources

The National Earthquake Information Center

The National Weather Service Forecast Office in Denver, Colorado

Jim H. Nishimine, M.D., FACOG, is a physician in private practice in Berkeley, California, and is Clinical Professor of Obstetrics-Gynecology at the University of California San Francisco.

Doug Noll, Esq., a professional mediator and peacemaker, has been in professional practice for 40 years. The author of *De-Escalate*, he has worked with Fortune 500 companies to help them understand the emotional and biological origins of human conflict. www.dougnoll.com

The Pennsylvania Public Utility Commission

Russell Quimby is a rail safety consultant and former Investigator-In-Charge of the Mechanical, Track, and Operations Investigation Groups at the National Transportation Safety Board, where he oversaw railroad and rail-transit accidents. He is a licensed locomotive operator and instructor. www.quimbyconsultingllc.weebly.com

www.Ready.gov

The Chief Consultant of Real World Rescue

Tim Richardson is a Professor at Seneca College and the University of Toronto specializing in cybersecurity, electronic fraud, and digital commerce. www.witiger.com

Dr. Lynn Rogers is a wildlife research biologist at Minnesota's Wildlife Research Institute and a Director of the North American Bear Center in Ely, Minnesota.

David Rose is the author of *Enchanted Objects: Design, Human Desire, and the Internet of Things*, a lecturer at the MIT Media Lab, and the founder of Ambient Devices. He is Vice President of Vision Technology at Warby Parker. www.enchantedobjects.com

Charles Schack is a retired New Hampshire State Trooper and has been an accident reconstructionist for 30 years, working with insurance companies and attorneys. He has personally handled hundreds of serious and fatal crashes, and analyzed 6,000 accidents. www.crashexperts.com

Greta Schanen, the Executive Editor of *Sailing Magazine*, has extensive offshore sailing experience, both racing and cruising.

Jeremy Sherman, PhD, MPP, is a "psycho-proctologist" who writes for *Psychology Today* and AlterNet, and has taught college courses in numerous social sciences.

Tim Smalley is a former boating and safety specialist at the Minnesota DNR; the U.S. Army's Cold Regions Research and Engineering Lab.

Will Stewart, an expert on photonics, communication, and electromagnetics, is a Fellow of the Institution of Engineering and Technology and the Royal Academy of Engineering in the U.K., and the Optical Society of America.

Zeb Tate, an Associate Professor of Electrical and Computer Engineering at the University of Toronto, focuses on improving the reliability of the power grid by leveraging new metering and processor technologies.

Andy Torbet, filmmaker and stuntman, spent 10 years in the British Special Forces as a paratrooper, diver, and bomb disposal officer. www.andytorbet.com

The U.S. Geological Survey

U.S. Department of Health and Human Services

Vicky Valtz is Chief Flight Instructor for Horizon Aviation, a flight school in New England, where she has taught for 10 years. She lives on an airpark in Cape Cod and commutes to work by plane. www.horizonaviation.com

Jon Van Horn, PA-C, a Trauma Physician Assistant in Portland, Oregon, has been deployed in the military multiple times over the past 26 years.

Dave Welch, President of the Institute of Explosives Engineers, owns Ramora UK, one of the world's leading explosive ordnance disposal companies

Mike Wilbanks is owner of Wilbanks Captive Bred Reptiles.

Tim Williams of Orlando's Gatorland has worked with alligators for nearly 30 years and trained other alligator wrestlers.

Jim Winburn is the director and stunt coordinator for two amusement park shows: "Batman" and the "Butch & Sundance Western Show."

Dr. Guy Windsor is a consulting swordsman, author, founder of The School of European Swordsmanship, and creator of the medieval combat card game Audatia. He specializes in researching and recreating medieval and Renaissance Italian swordsmanship. www.guywindsor.net/blog/

Melissa Zimdars, PhD, is co-editor of *Fake News: Understanding Media and Misinformation in the Digital Age* (MIT Press) and an Assistant Professor of Communication at Merrimack College.

Al Zulich is the Director of the Harford Reptile Breeding Center in Bel Air, Maryland.

ABOUT THE AUTHORS

JOSHUA PIVEN has been chased by knife-wielding motorcycle bandits (he escaped); stranded on a chairlift during a howling blizzard (he was rescued); and once had a kidney stone (he passed it). He lives in Philadelphia. **www.joshuapiven.com**

DAVID BORGENICHT has thus far survived rattlesnake, bear, and mountain lion encounters (well, viewings anway), muggings, con artists, and his own teenage children. He lives in Philadelphia and is the founder of Quirk Books. **www.quirkbooks.com**

Visit **www.worstcasescenario.com** for new scenarios, updated info, expert Q&As, and more!